OHIO'S TROY vs. PIQUA FOOTBALL RIVALRY

THE BATTLE ON THE MIAMI

DAVID FONG

Published by The History Press
Charleston, SC 29403
www.historypress.net

Copyright © 2015 by David Fong
All rights reserved

Front cover, top right: Courtesy of Troy High School.
All other cover images courtesy of Lee Woolery/Speedshot Photo.

First published 2015

Manufactured in the United States

ISBN 978.1.62619.782.4

Library of Congress Control Number: 2015943182

Notice: The information in this book is true and complete to the best of our knowledge. It is offered without guarantee on the part of the author or The History Press. The author and The History Press disclaim all liability in connection with the use of this book.

All rights reserved. No part of this book may be reproduced or transmitted in any form whatsoever without prior written permission from the publisher except in the case of brief quotations embodied in critical articles and reviews.

CONTENTS

Preface	5
Introduction	11
1. The Early Years: 1899–1924	19
2. Wertz Arrives at Piqua: 1925–1951	25
3. Everyone's All-Americans: 1952–1968	32
4. The Greatest Story Ever Told: 1969–1983	40
5. Troy and Piqua, Back on Top: 1984–1991	47
6. Nolan vs. Nees	56
7. The Games of the Century: 1992	61
8. The Golden Age: 1990–1999	72
9. To the Present: 2000–2014	84
10. Legends of the Fall: Piqua's Greatest Players	110
11. Legends of the Fall: Troy's Greatest Players	122
Troy vs. Piqua Scores	137
Index	139
About the Author	144

PREFACE

I'll never forget the first time I fell in love.

It was a night that began much like most other nights for me in high school—with my best friend, Eric Hughes, picking me up at my house in his parents' metallic green Buick. Since I didn't have a car, I was reliant on him to get me wherever I needed to go.

This night, however, was special.

As we hurtled up County Road 25-A—Hughes was known for driving at a high rate of speed wherever we needed to go—toward Piqua's old Wertz Stadium (which once housed some of the most powerful teams in Piqua High School football history but has since become a soccer facility), we had no idea what was about to transpire.

It was a warm September night in 1991, and I was a senior at Troy High School. The Troy and Piqua football teams—both undefeated at the time—were about to play for the 106th time. Although we got to the stadium several hours before kickoff, the stands on both sides of the field were near capacity. By the time the game finally started at 7:30 p.m.—nearly two hours after we had arrived—fans from both sides were in full throat. The two teams battled back and forth, with Piqua eventually pulling out a 24–6 victory.

Something special happened that night. I went to the game hoping for a Troy victory, figuring it might be the last time I saw a Troy-Piqua game before I left for college. Surrounded by my classmates—and somewhere in the neighborhood of eight thousand other screaming fans—I realized this was more than just a football game.

PREFACE

Piqua's captains line up for the coin toss in 2011. *Courtesy of Lee Woolery/Speedshot Photo.*

That night, I fell in love with the rivalry. Growing up in Troy, I had attended other matchups between the Trojans and Indians before, but this night was special. I knew, deep down, that I would never miss another Troy-Piqua game. And to this day, more than two decades later, I have not.

That night, Ohio's most-played high school football rivalry game became my passion. Actually, the word "passion" may not be enough. To those who know me best, the word "obsession" would probably be more fitting. I have spent my entire adult life following the rivalry, studying both sides, learning about the great players, coaches and moments. When the opportunity to write a book about the Troy-Piqua rivalry arose, I knew it was a chance to fulfill a yearning I had carried with me for decades.

This book would not have been possible without the help of so many people along the way.

Right around the same time I was discovering my love for the rivalry, I discovered my passion for writing. For that, I thank my high school English teachers, Mrs. Barbara Wannemacher, Mr. Chris Davis and Mrs. Diane Grimes-Bogner. They taught me how to find my voice through writing.

That same year I started writing in earnest, I also started working part time for the *Troy Daily News*, answering phones in the sports department. If my high school English teachers taught me how to find my voice, the

PREFACE

"The Battle on the Miami" trophy, awarded to the winner of the Troy-Piqua game. *Courtesy of Lee Woolery/Speedshot Photo.*

PREFACE

Troy Daily News gave me the platform to use it. I would work at the *TDN* all though my final year in high school and my four-plus years at The Ohio State University. I began working full time at the *TDN* immediately following my graduation from Ohio State in 1996. Thank you to Bill Begley, Kevin Aprile, Steve Jacoby, David Lindeman, Nancy Bowman and Joel Walker for taking a chance on me and giving me a daily platform from which to write. Thank you to my current TDN family for all of their help and support.

Thank you to everyone at The Ohio State University—and all my *Lantern* co-workers—for encouraging me and giving me the strength to continue writing when I was still a confused kid trying to find my place in this world.

Thank you to the people who helped me put together the nuts and bolts of the book you hold in your hand. Thank you to the dozens of former players and coaches for letting me be a part of your lives for the past two decades. Thank you for taking the time to let me pester you with interviews during the biggest, most important week of the football season. A special thanks to former Troy coaches Steve Nolan and Scot Brewer and current

Troy quarterback Matt Barr looks for an open receiver during the 2014 meeting between the two teams. *Courtesy of Lee Woolery/Speedshot Photo.*

PREFACE

The Great American Rivalry Series Trophy, awarded to the winner of the Troy-Piqua game. *Courtesy of Lee Woolery/Speedshot Photo.*

Piqua coach Bill Nees, the men who never once squelched an overzealous reporter looking for a new angle on the rivalry. Thank you for letting me tell your stories.

Thanks to Troy historian Patrick Kennedy for his constant help with fact-checking and perspective. Thank you to Lee Woolery and Paul Delwiche for

PREFACE

providing the beautiful photos you find in this book. Thank you to former Trojan and current Troy attorney John Fulker for guiding me through the contract process.

Thank you to my parents and brothers and sisters for helping an unathletic, nerdy kid be a part of an athletic family and helping me realize just how important sports can be.

And, most of all, thank you to my wife, Michelle, and our two children, Sophie and Max. Thank you for being my constant source of inspiration and strength. Without the three of you, I wouldn't have gotten this far in life—and realizing my dream of writing a book about the greatest rivalry in high school sports would never have happened.

INTRODUCTION

All Benson McGillvary was looking for was salvation. For himself. For his team. For the season. For a town.

And when the Troy junior cradled the 2-point conversion pass from quarterback Tyler Wright in his arms—giving the Troy football team an improbable 36–35 win over rival Piqua at Troy Memorial Stadium that October 19, 2007 night—he found it.

Salvation poured over the six-foot, one-inch, 165-pound McGillvary, washing away the angst he'd been feeling for six weeks since blowing a coverage on defense late in the game against Sidney, allowing the Yellowjackets to escape with a 17–14 win in the third week of the season.

"I felt like I let my team down," McGillvary said of the loss to Sidney in a *Troy Daily News* interview following the game. "I didn't do my job. It was the worst feeling I've ever had in my entire life. But I knew I was going to come back and redeem myself. I knew I was going to help my team win a game this year—I just never dreamed it would have been the Piqua game."

Not many people did.

That year, Piqua was heavily favored to dismantle the Trojans, much as it had the year before. Piqua—on its way to a Division II state football championship—had simply run over its rival in 2006, outscoring the Trojans 42–7.

The following year, Piqua had lost some of its top talent—namely Mr. Football Ohio running back Brandon Saine, who had since moved on to play at The Ohio State University—but still returned enough to make a playoff

INTRODUCTION

Troy fans cheer on the Trojans during the 2012 game. *Courtesy of Lee Woolery/Speedshot Photo.*

run. The Indians entered the game 7-1, while Troy came in struggling at 3-5 and on a three-game losing streak. On that night, however, there was magic in the air for the Trojans.

As expected, Piqua jumped out to a 14–0 lead and appeared, for all intents and purposes, on its way to routing its rival for a second straight year. The Trojans came roaring back, however, behind running back Corey Brown.

Brown forever etched himself into the rivalry's lore that night, carrying the ball forty-five times—yes, forty-five times—for 317 yards and four touchdowns. Behind an offensive line that included future college players Jake Current (Wisconsin) and T.J. White (Wofford), Brown evoked images of legendary Troy running backs such as Bob Ferguson, Gordon Bell and Ryan Brewer.

And he did it on the biggest stage of them all.

After Brown's third touchdown of the night had tied the game at 28, however, Piqua's Ryan Musselman returned the ensuing kickoff for a touchdown, and Wes Reed booted the extra point, giving the Indians a 35–28 lead.

With 6:31 left to play, Troy took over deep in its own territory and, with Brown leading the way, put together a fourteen-play drive that ate more than six minutes off the clock. With less than a minute to play, Brown punched in his fourth touchdown of the night, cutting Piqua's lead to 35–34.

INTRODUCTION

Troy quarterback Tyler Wright lines up against Piqua in 2008. *Courtesy of Lee Woolery/ Speedshot Photo.*

And that's when Troy decided to go for two.

"We figured we had nothing to lose," Troy coach Steve Nolan said. "We were the underdog."

With Brown suffering from severe leg cramps, the Trojans put the ball in the hands of Wright, who dropped back to pass and almost immediately was hit by a Piqua defender. As he was falling down, Wright flipped the ball to McGillvary, who was crushed by Piqua linebacker David Rolf, who would go on to play college football at Michigan State University the following year.

McGillvary held on to the ball, giving the Trojans one of the most memorable wins in a rivalry that has played itself out 130 times, more than any other in Ohio high school football history.

As incredible as that night was, however, it's one of just hundreds of magical moments between the two schools. Troy and Piqua first played in

INTRODUCTION

Getting mohawks the week of the game is an annual tradition for both teams, this time during the 2011 season. *Courtesy of Lee Woolery/Speedshot Photo.*

Troy and Piqua battle at the line of scrimmage in 2011. *Courtesy of Lee Woolery/Speedshot Photo.*

INTRODUCTION

1899. That year, the Indians defeated the Trojans twice, 17–0 and 7–5. Since then, the two schools have met 128 more times, with the rivalry currently sitting at a 62-62-4 standstill entering the 2015 season.

For more than a century, the two teams have battled back and forth—much like they did that October night in 2007. And much like that 123rd meeting between the two teams, the series has whipsawed, with one team seemingly taking control, only to see the opposing team battle back and even up the rivalry.

From Piqua's dominance under the late George "Buck" Wertz in the 1920s, '30s and '40s to Troy taking over under head coach Lou Juillerat in the 1950s,

Troy and Piqua playing in the snow in 2014. *Courtesy of Lee Woolery/Speedshot Photo.*

INTRODUCTION

to the near-even "Golden Age" of the rivalry under Troy coach Steve Nolan and Piqua coach Bill Nees in the 1980s, '90s and into the current century, the Troy-Piqua rivalry has remained almost inexplicably even. It's almost as if both teams simply refuse to let the other take a commanding lead.

And all the drama has taken place under the watchful eyes of both Miami County communities. Over the years, the rivalry has become something

Troy fans get ready for the game in 2014. *Courtesy of Lee Woolery/Speedshot Photo.*

INTRODUCTION

Troy players break through the banner prior to the Troy-Piqua game in 2009. *Courtesy of Lee Woolery/Speedshot Photo.*

much more than a high school football game; it has become the social event of the season, a place to see and be seen. It is a de facto high school reunion for both schools, as alumni from both schools pack the stands every year to see the rivalry renewed.

When the two undefeated, state-ranked teams met in 1992, an estimated fourteen thousand fans—combined, the two communities boast somewhere in the neighborhood of forty thousand residents—packed their way into Troy Memorial Stadium to see the two teams play. Think about that—more than a quarter of the population between the two cities came to watch a high school football game.

For the thousands of players who have participated in the rivalry, it's become much more than a game; it's become something they'll never forget for the rest of their lives. Few of the players who have ever participated in the rivalry have gone on to play college football, while only a dozen between the two schools have gone on to play in the NFL.

For so many, the Troy-Piqua rivalry is the apex not only of their athletic careers but also of their childhoods.

"I still can't believe this," McGillvary said after the game. "I can't describe it. This is the best I've ever felt in my entire life."

He's not alone.

Chapter 1
THE EARLY YEARS

1899–1924

The bad blood between the cities of Troy and Piqua actually predates the football field. Piqua was founded in 1807, and seven years later, the city of Troy was incorporated. In the early days, it wasn't uncommon for residents of both towns to engage in skirmishes, some of which ultimately turned bloody.

Tensions between the two communities would come to a head later that century, however, as they eventually engaged in what has become known as the "Courthouse War."

Just as few structures in Miami County rise higher than the dome atop the Miami County Courthouse, few tales stand taller than the one surrounding the courthouse itself. The story of the "Courthouse War" begins in the early 1800s, when residents of Piqua—then known as Washington—began lobbying legislators for their town to become the Miami County seat. Washington leaders argued that not only did they have the larger town but also the swamps that surrounded Troy at the time were sure to make visitors ill. Troy residents countered that they should have the county seat because of Troy's more centralized location with the county.

State leaders elected to build the first Miami County Courthouse in Troy and would go on to build three more courthouses between 1803 and 1841. In 1887, county commissioners decided to build a new courthouse—and Piqua residents viewed that as one final chance to get the courthouse moved back to their city.

Piquads petitioned the state legislature and eventually got a commission from Columbus to come to Miami County to settle the dispute once and for all. According to legend, on the first day of the visit, legislators were given a tour of Piqua, where they were shown the town's size and prosperity—both of which, at the time, exceeded those of Troy. The next day, however, the Columbus visitors visited Troy, where they were treated to a banquet at the Lollis Hotel. The story goes that in addition to the banquet, the ones who would make the final decision were treated to a deep well of adult beverages, and the party lasted well into the night.

Apparently, the wining and dining paid off for Troy officials. By the time the hungover state officials left Miami County, their decision had been made. As a result, the courthouse stayed in Troy.

That wasn't the end of the rivalry, however. When the statue of Lady Justice was placed atop the courthouse dome, she was placed with her posterior facing Piqua—on purpose. "Madam Justice looks past Troy to the towns of Tippecanoe and West Milton, while she turns her bustle in the direction of Piqua," an editor of the *Tippecanoe Herald* wrote in 1887.

For more than two hundred years, the two cities have continued to battle over everything from business and industry to land usage. Beginning in 1899, they took it to the football field. Even then, however, there still was bloodshed.

Troy began its football program in 1897, playing Sidney twice and a team comprising alumni once. Two years later, Piqua—under the tutelage of Coach Edward Allen—began its program. It seemed only natural that the two schools would play each other. Considering how the second meeting in the history of the two schools turned out, it's surprising they continued the rivalry at all.

In the first of 130 meetings between the two schools, the Trojans defeated the Indians 17–0 in an otherwise un-noteworthy contest. The two teams would meet again later in the season, with Troy pulling out a 7–5 victory when it scored a safety in the game's final seconds.

Piqua fans attending the game—some of whom likely still were steaming at the way Troy had acquired the rights to the Miami County Courthouse a little more than a decade earlier—felt the game had been fixed by unscrupulous officials. Following the game, which was played at Midway Park in Troy, a riot broke out among the six hundred or so spectators. By the time the dust settled, bones had been broken and blood had been shed—all over a high school football game.

It wouldn't be the last time controversy would rear its head in the early days of the rivalry. In 1900, Troy and Piqua played three times in the same year, the only time in the history of the rivalry that has happened.

THE BATTLE ON THE MIAMI

The 1897 Troy High School football team. *Courtesy of the Troy Historical Library.*

Troy won the first game 2–0, while Piqua was victorious in the second game by a 26–0 score.

In an effort to break the stalemate that year, a third meeting between the two teams was arranged. Some historians have argued that the game was not a game between the two high schools but rather a contest arranged between two "city teams," which allowed both teams to use players who weren't exclusively high school students but were simply residents of both cities—or "ringers."

"The early years of these two football teams can be an adventure to figure out because of the lack of enforced rules, for example, the use of non–high school players; the lack of detail in early newspapers regarding the games—for example, few names are mentioned—and the 'progressive' schedule of games, for example, games were arranged and set up, then cancelled at the last minute for numerous reasons," Troy historian Patrick Kennedy said.

Troy won the third contest 16–0. In the years since, some historians have argued that since the third contest was a city game and not a game contested solely by high school players, it shouldn't count in the rivalry's tally and should be stricken from the record. If that were the case, the two teams actually have met 129 times, with Piqua leading the series 62-61-6.

The next year, in 1901, there is the possibility that the two teams again played three times. Details on a third game are so sketchy that even the two now-defunct Troy newspapers of the time, the *Buckeye* and the *Miami Union*, disagree about whether it was played.

The December 5, 1901 edition of the *Buckeye* states that the "Troy high school football team" played "the high school team from Piqua at Midway Park" on Thanksgiving afternoon (November 28, 1901). The competing newspaper in Troy, the *Miami Union*, states in its December 5 edition, however, that "the Troy High School Foot Ball Team went to Urbana on Thanksgiving Day and lost to the team of that city, 24–5." Papers from Troy, Piqua and Urbana side with the *Miami Union*. The *Urbana Daily Citizen* provides a detailed account of Urbana defeating Troy on Thanksgiving Day. The *Piqua Daily Call* gives the results of Piqua taking on Dayton Central in Piqua.

It bears mentioning, however, that both schools choose to continue to count the third 1900 game in the official tally. Many have joked it's one of the few things the two schools—or the two communities—have come to agree on. Neither school has recognized a third game played between the two teams in 1901 as part of the official tally.

Following the three-game series in 1900, Piqua would dominate the Trojans the next three years, winning four games by a combined total of 71–14. The two teams did not play each other from 1904 to 1908, one of the final two breaks in the continuous streak between the two schools.

In 1905, it took nothing short of an order by President Theodore Roosevelt to get the two teams to stop playing each other. That year, Troy played a one-

The 1907 Troy High School football team. *Courtesy of the Troy Historical Library.*

game season, thanks in large part to Roosevelt's decision to ban football in the United States.

Roosevelt banned football that season in an effort to curb what had become an incredibly violent sport, but he may actually have saved the sport in doing so. In the early days, the sport had very few rules and resembled a gang fight as much as a game. In 1905 alone, eighteen players across the nation died while playing in football games. So Roosevelt shut things down, rules were changed and added—most notably the forward pass, which eliminated the game's violent scrums—and football resumed the next year.

Troy and Piqua would resume play in 1909, with Troy winning the first of two contests, 17–5, and Piqua winning the second game by a 5–0 tally. The Trojans and Indians did not meet in 1910. It would be the last time in the history of the rivalry that the two teams did not play each other. Once the rivalry resumed in 1911, the two teams would play twice a year from that season until 1924.

The first three decades of the rivalry featured a brand of football that today's football fans would scarcely recognize. Even after President Roosevelt shut down the game and the forward pass was introduced in an effort to make the game less violent, both teams continued to rely heavily on the run game, which often led to low-scoring contests. One notable exception came in 1913, when the Trojans rolled to an 85–0 win over the Indians.

Still, though, the games—and the teams themselves—remained largely unorganized affairs. It wasn't uncommon for the two teams to cycle through

The 1913 Troy High School football team. *Courtesy of the Troy Historical Library.*

coaches, many of whom had little working knowledge of the intricacies of the relatively new game.

From 1899 to 1924, Piqua had nine different coaches and no coach at all in 1901. That year, the Indians were led by Manager Summers, a young man from the community. Troy would have eleven coaches during that same time frame, one of whom was Leslie "Prep" Wells, who both played for and coached the Trojans during his high school career. Wells would go on to play both football and baseball at The Ohio State University and was named to OSU's All-Decade Team for the 1900s.

With all of the coaching changes—and the lack of a true leader for either program—neither team would establish dominance during the early years of the rivalry. All of that would change in 1925, however, when Piqua hired a man named George "Buck" Wertz.

Chapter 2

WERTZ ARRIVES AT PIQUA

1925–1951

George Wertz completely changed the face of the Piqua-Troy rivalry for more than two decades. He became the head coach at Piqua in 1925, going 7-2-1 his first season, including a 20–6 victory over Troy in the final game of the season. That first year was merely a harbinger, as Wertz built the Indians into a powerhouse—one that would, quite simply, dominate Troy during his tenure. Wertz's Indians would win seven of their first eight matchups against Troy, outscoring the Trojans by a combined score of 121–33. During his career, Wertz faced the Trojans twenty-six times, going 17-6-3 against them, a winning percentage in the rivalry that puts him near the top of the rivalry for either team.

During his coaching career at Piqua, Wertz went 165-63-21. The Indians recorded just three losing seasons during that span, went undefeated three times and went undefeated and untied twice—this was before the playoff era, which meant a team could finish the season undefeated without winning a state championship—a feat unmatched by any Piqua coach since.

During his reign as head coach, the Indians would capture ten Miami Valley League (MVL) titles. During that same time frame, Troy would capture just two MVL crowns.

His record of 165 wins would stand as the school record for more than sixty years, until current Piqua coach Bill Nees surpassed him in 2014. So impressive was Wertz's legacy that even the man who surpassed him in career wins remains effusive in his praise for his predecessor. "George Wertz remains the coach against which all Piqua coaches will eventually be measured," Nees said. "He is really the one who put Piqua football on the map. He took the program from an unorganized group of players and coaches and made it what it is today. When you look back at the history of Piqua football, it's impossible for George Wertz not to be first on the list of people you talk about. When you look back at the numbers, it's pretty incredible what he was able to accomplish."

As good as Wertz was, he seemingly was at his best when the rival Trojans were playing well—only to have Wertz and his Indians ruin banner seasons. By the time Wertz took over the Piqua program in 1925, the Troy-Piqua game had been moved to the final game of the season. It frequently was played on Thanksgiving afternoon.

Five times during Wertz's tenure at Piqua, the Trojans entered the final game of the season with an unblemished record; four of those times, the Indians emerged with the win. In 1932, 1938, 1945 and 1947, Piqua was Troy's lone loss of the season. Only in 1946, when Troy finished the season 10-0 and won an MVL title, were the Trojans able to maintain a clean slate following the rivalry game.

1932: Piqua 9, Troy 6

Football often has been referred to as a "game of inches," but sometimes it's won by a foot—literally.

In a series that produced several "games of the century" during the 1900s, the first contest to earn that moniker was the 1932 matchup between the Trojans and the Indians. Troy came into the game as a slight favorite, boasting a 6-0-2 record and looking for just its second win over its rival since 1923. Piqua, meanwhile, entered the game with a 5-1-2 record. The Indians had captured three Miami Valley League titles in the past five years, while Troy still was in search of the first league title in school history.

The stage was set for a classic matchup—and despite the similar records, most still expected the Trojans to win. The year before, Piqua had scratched out a 13–12 victory over its rival. Troy had been favored in that game, too.

"Troy entered the game a big favorite and was leading, 12 to 0, until late in the game when the Indians caught the Trojans napping and punched over two touchdowns to win, 13 to 12," *Troy Daily News* sports columnist Jack Miller wrote of the 1931 game in a column previewing the 1932 contest. "The game left the Troy fans completely stunned for they had counted on a

THE BATTLE ON THE MIAMI

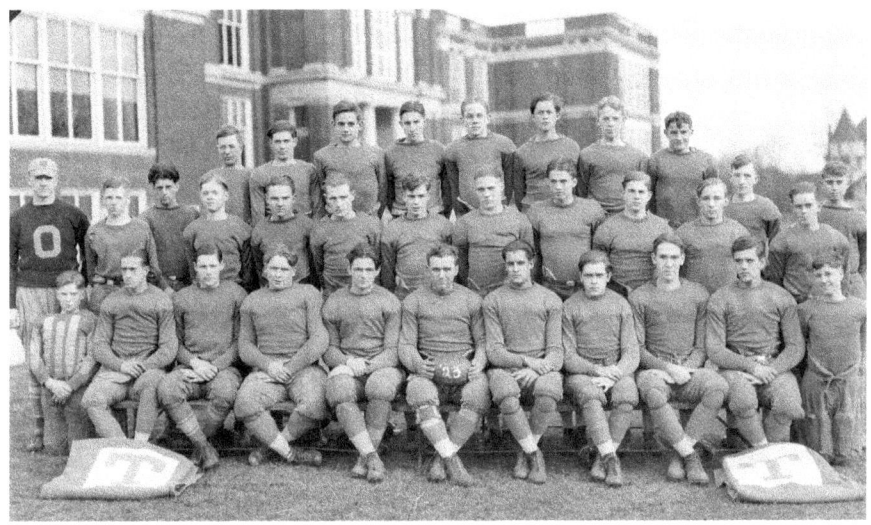

The 1923 Troy High School football team. *Courtesy of the Troy Historical Library.*

sure victory and on the past records of the two teams should have been right. But football is one sport that cannot be figured on past performances as has been so well illustrated this year."

Miller figured Troy would use the previous year's loss to Piqua as motivation in the 1932 game. "Personally, and this is no bung, we think Troy should win over the Indians, not by any large margin but they should win," he wrote. "We base this on several things, which we will set down here and now. In the first place, Troy has a superior line. From tackle to tackle, the Troy line outweighs the Indian forward wall 10 pounds to the man which means the Trojans ought to be able to push their opponents aside whenever necessary. In addition to their extra weight the Trojan forwards have displayed a game throughout the season that is superior to the Indians."

One thing Miller did not count on, however, was the ability of Wertz to get his team ready to play.

More than five thousand people showed up at Piqua's Roosevelt Field for the Thanksgiving Day game—a Troy-Piqua attendance record at the time. Heavy rains had turned the field into a veritable bog, and both teams struggled to move the ball. The muddy conditions essentially negated any advantage the Trojans had along the offensive line, as Troy's linemen were unable to gain ample footing to push around the Piqua line.

Troy took a 6–0 lead in the second quarter when halfback Tom Calloway was able to score on a one-yard plunge. Piqua would tie the score before halftime, however, on a touchdown run by Bill Bolton. Both teams would miss their extra point attempts following the touchdowns, leaving the score deadlocked at 6–6 for much of the rest of the afternoon.

The soupy field conditions would affect not only both offenses but both kicking games as well—until the game's final moments, that is. Piqua's Captain Purdy booted a field goal that easily cleared the crossbar, giving the Indians a 9–6 advantage, the final margin of victory, their fourth MVL title in six years and bragging rights in what was at that point the "Game of the Century."

Piqua would continue its dominance over the Trojans for the rest of the decade and into the early 1940s. Following the "Game of the Century" in 1932, Piqua would go 8-2-1 against the Trojans from 1933 to 1943.

In 1941, however, Troy did make a coaching change that would bring some parity to a lopsided rivalry when it hired Coach Carlton Kazmaier to lead the football team. In three decades of coaching at Troy, every athletic program Kazmaier touched seemed to turn to gold, whether it was football, basketball, golf or track and field. From 1940 to 1970, Kazmaier helped churn out champions in all four sports.

In 1941, he took over as head coach. From 1941 to 1951, Kazmaier's Troy football teams compiled a record of 73-27-6 (a .690 winning percentage), including four years in which the team went 36-3-1, won two conference championships and finished as a runner-up once.

Following a slow start the first four years under Kazmaier, the Trojans went 55-10-1 (.830) the final seven years. During that span, the Trojans outscored their opponents 202–24, including ten shutouts.

Under Kazmaier's leadership, Troy went 4-5-2 against the Indians from 1941 to 1951, and while the Indians continued to hold the edge in the series, Kazmaier was the first Troy coach to put a competitive product on the field against the Indians. In a quarter century of coaching, Wertz's teams lost to the Trojans only six times—but four of those losses came during the ten-year span in which Kazmaier was the Trojans' head coach.

Even with the improved effort against the Indians, however, Wertz's Piqua teams still seemed to have the advantage in the high-profile meetings between the two teams.

In a four-year span from 1945 to 1948, the Trojans lost just three games, two of which came against the Indians. In the final of those four meetings, the two teams played to a 0–0 tie. In 1945, Troy entered the game against the Indians with a 9-0 record and once again had its sights set on claiming the first league title in school history. Piqua entered the game 8-1 but thoroughly trounced the Trojans, 25–6, to claim its ninth MVL title under Wertz.

THE BATTLE ON THE MIAMI

The 1945 Troy High School football team. *Courtesy of the Troy Historical Library.*

Troy would gain a measure of revenge the following year, capping off a perfect 10-0 season with a 12–6 win over the Indians, securing the first MVL title in school history. That set up a rubber match between the two teams in 1947.

Troy would again enter the 1947 meeting with a perfect 9-0 record and a nineteen-game winning streak, seeking its second consecutive unblemished season and MVL crown. Piqua also would enter the game with a 9-0 mark, setting up the second "Game of the Century" in a fifteen-year span.

1947: Piqua 40, Troy 6

With both teams undefeated, fans flocked to Troy's Midway Park to get a seat for the game. The game would set a new attendance record as nearly nine thousand fans showed up to see the two undefeated teams play on a Friday night in Troy.

One fan couldn't wait for the day of the game to make sure she got the seat she wanted. According to a *Troy Daily News* report, Piqua resident Jeanne Spencer took a taxi to Troy, showing up for the game at 2:00 p.m. on Thursday. She was "well equipped with blankets, lunch and a radio and promptly posted herself on the grass outside the general admission gate." She, along with the thousands of Piqua fans who waited until game day to arrive, would not leave disappointed.

Unlike the first "Game of the Century," which was decided on a late field goal, Piqua would turn the second heralded contest between the two teams into a romp, blasting the Trojans 40–6.

"Troy's football castle tumbled about its ears Friday night when the Piqua Indians blasted the Trojans for a surprising and devastating 40 to 6 defeat that smashed Troy's 19-game winning streak and brought to Piqua its tenth Miami Valley League grid championship as well as an undefeated season," the *Troy Daily News* reported in its Saturday edition the next morning.

"The ease with which Piqua smashed Troy's hope for a second title stunned the Trojan rooters while the joyful Piqua followers could hardly believe their eyes. Close to 9,000 fans jammed the park for what they expected to be a hard and close battle. Instead they saw a demoralized Troy team absorb the worst defeat suffered by either team in their annual classic since the organization of the Miami Valley League."

The game was close early, as both teams were tied 6–6 after a Piqua touchdown early in the second quarter. From that point on, however, it was all Indians, as Piqua's defense shut down the Trojan offense. In the final three quarters, the Trojans crossed midfield just twice and never again advanced any farther than the Piqua thirty-two-yard line.

Piqua's defense continually harassed Troy quarterback Harold "Corky" Valentine, who would go on to greater fame as a pitcher for the Cincinnati Reds following his high school graduation.

The following year, in 1948, Troy would again have a superior team, but once again, the Indians would put a damper—albeit a much smaller one—on the Trojans' season. The two teams would play to a 0–0 tie. It was a moral victory for Piqua, which would finish the season 5-4-1. Troy, meanwhile, would finish the season 8-1-1 and claim a share of the MVL title. Still, a missed chance to end the season with a win over Piqua would serve as a black mark on an otherwise stellar season for the Trojans.

The next season was a banner year for the Trojans, as it was the first game played in the twelve-thousand-seat Troy Memorial Stadium. At the time, it was one of the largest high school stadiums in the state of Ohio, a monument built to honor war veterans and heavily financed by the esteemed Hobart family, which also had a hand in building Hobart Arena—the lone ice rink in Miami County—a public swimming pool and Miami Shores Golf Course.

THE BATTLE ON THE MIAMI

Troy, led by Bussie Favorite and Dick Carnes, the first one-thousand-yard rushers in school history, would beat Piqua 20–3 in the first game between the two ever played at Troy Memorial Stadium. Favorite—known literally and figuratively as "the Man Who Built Troy Memorial Stadium," as he was the first major individual star in Troy history and worked on the construction of the stadium the summer before his senior year—ran for three touchdowns in that game.

Fittingly, however, Wertz's Indians would defeat the Trojans 39–12 in the final game he coached between the two rivals. Following his retirement, the football stadium in downtown Piqua would eventually be renamed Wertz Stadium. The Indians would play there until the construction of Alexander Stadium/Purk Field in 2001.

As Wertz's coaching career came to an end, however, so, too, did the Indians' recent string of domination over their neighbors to the south. Soon after his retirement, Troy would see the arrival of its own coaching legend, Lou Juillerat, along with an influx of talent never before seen in school history. Those two factors would turn the rivalry in Troy's favor for the next generation.

Chapter 3
EVERYONE'S ALL-AMERICANS

1952–1968

High school football coaches are forced to play the hands they are dealt. Sure, a talented coach can turn good talent into great teams and transform an average football player into a very good one. In general, though, true superstars are all about the luck of the draw. College coaches are afforded the opportunity to build their programs by picking and choosing the top recruits from across the nation. Coaches in the NFL can turn moribund teams around through smart draft choices and selective free agents. High school coaches, however, are forced to play the kids within their school district. Star players come and go—an All-Ohio lineman here, a two-thousand-yard rusher there. Sometimes, because it's all a crapshoot, that leads to "talent eclipses," in which coaches are forced to fill the gaps with marginal talents. Even at talent-rich programs such as Troy and Piqua, superstars usually come along once in a generation.

Except, of course, when they don't.

Following the retirement of Piqua coach George Wertz, the Troy football program put together a galaxy of star players that shone as bright as any group of players ever to compete in the Troy-Piqua rivalry. This assemblage of superstars led to the Trojans completely flipping the rivalry. If the 1920s, '30s and '40s belonged to the Indians, the 1950s and early '60s were almost the sole property of the Trojans.

How talented were the Trojans in the mid-1950s and early 1960s? Consider this: The four-year stretch from 1957 to 1960 saw Troy High School produce three future Division I college Americans, all of whom were both NFL and

THE BATTLE ON THE MIAMI

AFL draft picks; one Maxwell Trophy winner; and one Heisman runner-up. At one point, three former Troy players were in the starting lineup for Woody Hayes's powerhouse teams at The Ohio State University, a feat that had never been accomplished before and has scarcely been accomplished since. So impressive was Troy's firepower that other Troy players who went on to earn college scholarships and have impressive careers in their own right frequently were lost in the luster of Troy's shining stars.

Needless to say, all of that talent translated into plenty of wins for Troy in the annual football rivalry with Piqua. Following Wertz's retirement in 1950, Piqua would win two of the next three games in the series. After Troy picked up a 41–12 win in 1951, the Indians would defeat the Trojans 25–12 in 1952 and 6–0 in 1953.

All of that was about to change, however, with the arrival of two people in particular: Troy coach Lou Juillerat and fullback Bob Ferguson. Those two would change the face of the rivalry for the better part of the next decade.

Juillerat and Ferguson came to the rivalry at essentially the same time, like two stars shooting across the same night sky. Juillerat took over as Troy's coach in 1954, which also happened to be Ferguson's freshman year in high school. The two would become forever linked in Trojan lore.

Juillerat arrived at Troy High School following a coaching stint at Baldwin-Wallace University in Berea. His first season at Troy, the Trojans went 3-6. There were, however, a number of positives. The Trojans did defeat Piqua, 18–0 that season. And, of course, there was Ferguson.

Ferguson announced his presence to the Ohio high school football world in the second game of his career, pounding his way to three touchdowns in a 40–18 win over Monroe. Although Troy would struggle for much of the rest of the season, the

Legendary Troy coach Lou Juillerat, 1958. *Courtesy of Paul Delwiche/Troy High School.*

bullish fullback still finished his freshman campaign with 454 rushing yards and 75 total points.

And the best was yet to come.

Following that 3-6 season, Ferguson would not lose another game the rest of his high school career as the Trojans went a combined 27-0 and outscored opponents by an average score of 40.6–7.3.

During that stretch, Piqua fared no better than the rest of Troy's competition, as the Trojans outscored the Indians 133–12 during Ferguson's three years at Troy.

1956: Troy 41, Piqua 6

By the time the 1956 matchup between the Trojans and Indians rolled around, desperation had sunk in for the Indian faithful. It had been two years since the Indians had managed to even score a point against the Trojans, with Troy rolling to an 18–0 win in 1954 and a 48–0 whitewashing the following year.

Piqua fans, apparently, had their fill. The week of the 1957 Troy-Piqua game, a group of Piqua supporters had broken into the Troy locker room and scrawled the words "Piqua, beat Troy" in large letters on the locker room wall. Piqua coach Jack Bickel lined up a series of parades, pep rallies and guest speakers in an effort to motivate his troops.

Juillerat, meanwhile, chose to eschew such motivational ploys. "We'll do our celebrating after the game," he said in an interview with the *Troy Daily News*.

Besides, the Troy coach was saving his tricks for the game.

Troy began the 1956 game at Troy Memorial Stadium with a trick play that had become one of Juillerat's coaching staples: the onside kick. Troy's Max Urick—a standout end and linebacker who would go on to become athletic director at both Iowa State University and Kansas State University after his playing days at Troy and Ohio Wesleyan University—recovered the onside kick.

"We got into the practice of using the onside kick on almost every kickoff," Urick said in a 1985 interview with the *Troy Daily News*. "Other teams would worry so much about losing it that their worst fears would happen. They would lose it."

Following Urick's recovery, Ferguson scored soon after on an eight-yard run. Troy's "trick" play nearly backfired on the following kickoff, however, as the Indians recovered the ensuing onside kick and Piqua's Dave Stockman broke free on a twenty-two-yard touchdown run to tie the game at 6–6.

In the long run, however, it wouldn't much matter; Troy still had the five-foot, eleven-inch, 215-pound Ferguson on its side.

That night, the future two-time Ohio State All-American and Heisman runner-up in 1961 would pile up 270 rushing yards on just seventeen carries. Nearly one-third of his runs that night would result in touchdowns, as Ferguson accounted for five of Troy's seven touchdowns on runs of 80, 76, 21, 8 and 2 yards.

"It was so common for him to break loose like that," Urick said in the 1985 interview. "I'm really surprised that's all he had that night. The main thing I remember about Fergie is that when the ball was snapped, you better get the hell out of his way.

"He was a very quiet guy. He was very talented and he had tremendous strength. He was truly a man among boys. The rest of us, I don't think, we are good as people thought we were. Fergie made the rest of us all look good."

Including, some would argue, Juillerat.

After losing six games that first year at Troy, Juillerat lost just five games in his final six years at Troy. In seven games against the Indians, he was 6-1, with the lone loss coming in 1958, as the Indians defeated the Trojans 14–6 the year after Ferguson graduated.

That one loss to Piqua turned out to be merely a blip on the radar during Juillerat's coaching tenure at Troy. Soon after Ferguson—along with fellow stars Gabe Hartman (who went on to play guard at Ohio State), Ron Houck (a defensive halfback at Ohio State) and Ron Stoner (a defensive halfback at Florida)—graduated, the next wave of Trojan legends already was enrolled at Troy.

Perhaps the greatest testament to Juillerat's coaching legacy was his ability to tailor his game plan to the personnel he had on hand. Sure, he looked like a genius when his offensive philosophy consisted of handing the ball off to Ferguson and watching him churn through opposing offenses. But what would happen when Ferguson was gone?

Simple enough—Juillerat changed his entire offense to suit the next two stars in his system, the "Tommy Guns."

Tom Myers and Tom Vaughn have remained friends well into their seventies. Although they live on opposite sides of the country—Myers currently resides in North Carolina, while Vaughn is retired and living in Arizona—they still keep in touch as often as possible and see each other whenever the opportunity presents itself. It's a friendship that was forged on the football field.

Just two years after Ferguson graduated, the next set of Trojan legends was ready to take flight—literally. If Troy had earlier won games by chewing up turf behind the hard-charging Ferguson, it won games with Myers and Vaughn by taking to the air. More than fifty years after graduating from Troy High School, the two remain the most prolific passing and receiving duo in school history.

"We always felt like we had a tradition to uphold," Vaughn said. "We knew Troy had great teams when Bobby Ferguson was there—we wanted to continue that legacy. Coach Juillerat was a great coach, and we didn't want any part of letting him down or diminishing his legacy at Troy."

And they didn't. In their final two years at Troy, they rewrote the record book. Myers still holds nearly every major passing record at Troy, while Vaughn holds nearly every receiving record. During their three years playing for Troy's varsity, the two combined to lead the Trojans to a 23-5 record.

After losing to Piqua as sophomores, Myers and Vaughn would lead the Trojans to blowout victories as juniors and seniors, defeating the Indians 20–0 in 1959 and by a whopping 62–0 score in 1960.

"We always wanted to beat that team eight miles north of Troy," Myers said. "To this day, I still don't say that city's name. That's how important winning that game was to us."

Myers would go on to earn All-American honors as a quarterback at Northwestern University, while Vaughn would become an All-American at Iowa State University. The two would be reunited again in the NFL, as both were drafted by the AFL's Denver Broncos and NFL's Detroit Lions. They would both end up playing for the Lions in the NFL. While Myers's stay in the NFL was brief, Vaughn would establish himself as a fearsome defensive back and kick returner for the Lions. He was named to Detroit's 50th Anniversary Team.

Eventually, however, all good things had to come to an end for the Trojans. Troy's unprecedented run of future All-Americans would come to an end following the graduation of Myers and Vaughn. Juillerat would leave with the dynamic duo, taking a college coaching job at Marietta College in the fall of 1961.

Even with the departure of Juillerat and Troy's cast of legends, however, Troy's string of victories over the Indians would continue for another three years, as the Trojans beat the Indians 12–6, 20–16 and 28–26.

Piqua finally would manage to stem the Trojans' tide, however, in 1964. Not coincidentally, that run by the Trojans would come to an end right around the same time Coach Chuck Asher arrived in Piqua.

It didn't take Chuck Asher long to realize just how much the Troy-Piqua rivalry meant to both communities. If he had any doubts, they were quickly cleared up in his first meeting with administrators after being named the Indians' new head coach.

"When I was hired, I was talking with the superintendent one day about buying a house…all that good stuff," Asher said in a 1985 interview with the *Troy Daily News*. "He told me not to unpack my bags until after the Troy game. It was all in a kidding fashion, of course. But there was something about the way he said it that let me know he was about half serious."

It was a message the new Piqua coach would take to heart.

Asher immediately turned the series back in Piqua's favor, winning his first five games against the Trojans: 20–0 in 1964, 28–16 in 1965, 8–6 in 1966, 34–6 in 1967 and 38–20 in 1968. He would go 17-2 his first two years at Piqua, winning a pair of MVL crowns. And after a decade of Trojan dominance, Asher gave Piqua fans—and players—something to believe in again.

"Obviously my football career started in large part thanks to Chuck Asher," said Dr. Dave Gallagher, a standout defensive tackle at Piqua who would go on to become an All-American at the University of Michigan and play in the NFL for the Chicago Bears and New York Giants before beginning his medical career, in an 2014 interview with the *Piqua Daily Call*. "He had just come to the school when I was in the sixth grade and he brought a new life and new spirit to the program. Right off the bat, he made the program into a winner. He was the kind of coach that you wanted to play for, that you wanted to please."

1964: Piqua 20, Troy 0

As successful as Asher was right off the bat in the rivalry game against Troy—and as well known as he would become for calling trick plays during his fifteen-year coaching career at Piqua—he can't claim responsibility for one of the greatest calls in his involvement with the game.

In his first contest against the Trojans in 1964, Troy took the opening kickoff and drove from its own fifteen-yard line down to the Piqua eight. Troy's drive stalled, however, when quarterback Bob Zimpher—subbing for injured quarterback Mark Goldner, who would go on to spend more than thirty years as Troy's boys' and girls' tennis coach—slipped out of the grasp of halfback Roger Shoup on fourth down.

Piqua's drive also stalled, however, and the Indians lined up to punt on fourth-and-three from the Indians' fifteen. What happened next surprised everyone at Troy Memorial Stadium—including Asher.

Piqua punter Mike Ostendorf—who also was the Indians' quarterback—took the snap and ran sixteen yards for a first down. "Mike did that one on his own," Asher said in an interview after the game.

The fake punt helped spark Piqua's first score of the game—and gave the Indians momentum they would ride the rest of the night. Following the fake punt, Keith Cummins broke loose on a forty-three-yard run to set up a six-yard touchdown run by Tom Lyman. Lyman also ran in the 2-point conversion, giving the Indians an 8–0 lead they would never lose.

"The fake punt was, in reality, a bad snap," Ostendorf said in a 1985 interview with the *Troy Daily News*. "We had several of those that particular year. That might have been the first one. We were fortunate it worked to our advantage."

It also was a matter of personal satisfaction and redemption for Ostendorf. Two years prior, Ostendorf—then just a sophomore quarterback in the midst of a string of Troy victories—showed up to school during Troy week to find a ketchup-splattered effigy of himself waiting in the principal's office. He was the obvious victim of overzealous Troy pranksters. "He [the principal] told me it was hanging from the flagpole that morning," Ostendorf said.

Piqua added to its lead in the third quarter when Ostendorf connected with Lyman on a fifty-seven-yard touchdown pass, stretching the Indians' lead to 14–0. Lyman added a final touchdown to ice the game.

"We had a good season my junior year, but it seemed we always found a way to lose," Lyman said. "By the time we were seniors, many of us had played together for a long time, and we finally got the opportunity to win some games."

Ostendorf was quick to give credit to Asher for the turnaround. "He changed the offense around entirely," he said. "We were poor in just about every athletic area my junior year, but the next year we wound up 9-1 in football and won the league."

For Asher, that first contest served as the perfect introduction to the rivalry. "The thing I remember about that game was the tremendous hype all the week before," he said in a *TDN* interview. "I had never seen a community rivalry as intense as Troy-Piqua was at that time. The thing that increased it even more was that Piqua thought it had a chance to win for the first time in a long time."

If Juillerat was known for producing superstars on offense before him, Asher become known for churning out defensive stars during his tenure, in particular Gallagher and defensive back Craig Clemons, who never lost to Troy during his playing days from 1964 to 1967. Following his career at Piqua, Clemons would go on to become an All-American at the University of Iowa and play six years for the Chicago Bears.

"I learned everything I needed to know about the game of football while I was at Piqua," Clemons said in a 2014 interview with the *Piqua Daily Call*. "I understood the gameplan and was receptive to change. I learned a lot from Coach Asher and Coach Dick Pearson. All in all, Piqua was the perfect situation for me as an athlete, too."

Following Piqua's 38–20 win over Troy in 1968, it seemed as though the Indians might never lose to the Trojans again. Under Asher, Piqua had never lost to its rival, peeling off five wins in a row. Piqua also was set to return a defense led by Gallagher the following year, while Troy would enter 1969 on the heels of a woeful 2-8 season.

What no one knew at the time, however, was that the rivalry was about to turn again—and one of the greatest stories in rivalry history was about to be told.

Chapter 4
THE GREATEST STORY EVER TOLD

1969–1983

After getting passed over for the third time, Jim Conard was ready to take his talents elsewhere—anywhere but Troy.

It was the fall of 1967, and Conard—a longtime assistant coach at Troy—had reached his breaking point. Since the departure of Lou Juillerat following the 1960 season, the Trojans had hired three coaches in five years, and each time, Conard felt he was the right man for the job, only to see the position go to someone else.

Troy had defeated rival Piqua the first three years after Juillerat had left to take the head coaching job at Marietta College, but since Chuck Asher's arrival in 1964, the Indians had defeated the Trojans every year. And Conard had his fill.

"I was about ready to tell the board [of education] what they could do with their coaching job," Conard said. "I felt like I should be the head coach, but they kept giving the job to someone else. By 1967, it was my third year as an assistant coach under Allen Richards, and I felt like it was time to move on with my career and go somewhere else."

That fall, however, a chance visit to a Troy Junior High School eighth grade game changed the course of Conard's coaching career—and forever changed the landscape of the Troy-Piqua rivalry, adding a story that has forever become a part of the rivalry's lore.

"That fall, I just happened to be at one of Troy's eighth grade games," Conard said. "Troy's eighth grade team had a kid named Gordon Bell. Every time he touched the ball, he scored a touchdown. I think he scored

THE BATTLE ON THE MIAMI

something like five touchdowns that day—three of them on punt returns. No one could tackle him. It was one of the most amazing things I had ever seen. That's when I figured, 'Maybe I need to stick around and be a part of this. I think something special is about to happen.'"

It was a prescient moment for Conard and a touchstone moment for the Troy High School football team—big changes were on the way.

Had Bell been the only star-in-waiting in that class, it would have been one thing. On the contrary, however, the Trojans were quietly putting together an assemblage of talent that would rival any in the history of the Troy-Piqua rivalry.

In addition to Bell, who would go on to earn All–Big Ten and All-American honors at the University of Michigan before a career in the NFL with the New York Giants and St. Louis Cardinals, his graduating class also featured linebacker/fullback Joe Allen, who would go on to play at the University of Florida; defensive tackle Dave Starkey, who would join Allen at Florida; halfback/safety Randy Walker, who would play at Miami University before beginning a coaching career that would eventually take him to Northwestern University; receiver Elmo Boyd, who would play at Eastern Kentucky University and in the NFL with the San Francisco 49ers and Green Bay Packers; and quarterback Al Mayer, who would go on to play at Marshall University. All told, twenty players from the 1972 graduating class would go on to play college football. The 1973 class that graduated a year behind Bell and his teammates, meanwhile, would send nearly a dozen players on to the college ranks.

"When Gordon and Walker and Starkey and Allen and all those guys were seniors, I used to say that the only teams in Ohio that could beat us that year were the Cleveland Browns, the Cincinnati Bengals and Ohio State," Conard said. "Maybe Miami University or Bowling Green could have given us a game that year…but I'm not even sure about that."

That talented class of 1972 would lay in wait its freshman year in 1968, as most of the members played freshman or junior varsity football. That fall, Piqua would defeat Troy, 38–20, behind a defense that included future college All-Americans Craig Clemons and Dave Gallagher.

That would be Richards's final season at Troy, as the Trojans finished the season 2-8. Conard would finally get his chance to take over in the offseason.

The trap was set.

OHIO'S TROY VS. PIQUA FOOTBALL RIVALRY

1969: Troy 22, Piqua 6

By the time the 1969 season rolled around, Troy and Piqua had gone their separate ways in terms of league alignments. Troy had since moved to the Western Ohio League, while Piqua had remained in the Miami Valley League. That led to a scheduling quirk that saw the rivalry game moved from its traditional spot in the middle or end of the season to the first game of the year, as both teams finished their seasons playing against their respective league schedules.

That move would turn out to be to Troy's advantage in 1969, as Piqua returned two key seniors in the backfield, while Troy entered the game with the largely unheard-of Bell, a sophomore, in the backfield.

Unheard of for exactly one play, that is.

On the first play of the 1969 season against rival Piqua, Bell took a simple handoff and turned it into a play that would set the tone for the next three seasons of the Troy-Piqua rivalry.

"It was a 13," Bell said in an interview with the *Troy Daily News*. "It was just a quick dive."

Bell turned that quick dive into a sixty-eight-yard touchdown run on the game's opening play, stunning the Piqua defense and announcing his arrival to the Ohio high school football world.

"I was just running scared," Bell told the *TDN* after the game. "On that first play, [Chris] White and [Tom] Wise blew that tackle and that linebacker right out of there. The rest was easy for me."

As things would turn out, the rest of the night would be easy for him. Bell finished his debut evening with three touchdowns and 173 rushing yards.

"When he was a sophomore, we knew he was going to be outstanding," Asher said in a 1985 interview with the *Troy Daily News*. "His performance that year didn't give us a whole lot to look forward to."

While the backfield of Bell and Allen was gashing the Indians, Troy's defense shut down Piqua's massive backfield of Gallagher and Scott Underwood. Again, the Trojans relied largely on the element of surprise to stop Piqua's heralded rushing duo. In the win the year before, Underwood had rushed for three touchdowns against the Trojans. In 1969, they found the sledding a little tougher, thanks in large part to a defensive adjustment Conard had cooked up for the game.

"The defense was basically a gap-eight," Conard said in an interview with the *Troy Daily News*. "We did not show it at all in our scrimmages. They had a lot of trouble blocking it."

THE BATTLE ON THE MIAMI

Conard's gap-eight defense put a defender in every gap along the line of scrimmage. The Trojans basically conceded the pass to the Indians in an effort to stop the bullish 220-pound Gallagher and 205-pound Underwood. The gamble paid off, as Piqua's lone pass attempt on the night fell incomplete, while Gallagher and Underwood combined to rush for just 103 yards and no scores.

"They were so big then, the only weakness we could see was that they had an inexperienced quarterback who wasn't very accurate throwing the ball," Conard said. "In my three years at Troy, that's the only time I ever used that defense."

It was a ploy that certainly caught the Indians by surprise.

"We were supposed to overpower them," Underwood said in a later interview. "We'd beaten them the last two years and they came up that season pretty much unheralded. They shut us down pretty well. They shot the gaps on every play. I honestly think that defense won the ballgame."

Having Bell in the backfield didn't hurt, either.

"Troy hadn't been playing very well against Piqua up to that time," Bell said. "The guys in my class felt we had a lot to prove. We wanted something we could talk about when we were older."

Over the course of three years, Bell would create something people still talk about more than forty years later. He would add touchdown runs of thirty-three and eighteen yards that night. Piqua's lone score came when David Jones returned the kickoff seventy-seven yards for a touchdown after Bell's final touchdown late in the game.

As good as Bell was that night, however, it was just the beginning. As a junior, he would score four touchdowns and rush for 324 yards in Troy's 54–6 win in the season opener. As a senior, he would rush for three touchdowns and pile up 212 rushing yards as Troy again whipped the Indians, this time by a final score of 36–6.

In three games against the Indians, Bell rushed for ten touchdowns and more than seven hundred yards. By the time he was finished, Asher had seen about enough of Troy's speedy halfback. So glad was Asher to see Bell graduate in the spring of 1972 that he made a proposition that has become one of the largest legends in the rivalry's history: he offered to personally present Bell with his diploma at the school's commencement ceremonies that spring.

"Absolutely, that happened," Bell said with a laugh. "He never actually showed up and did it, but the offer was on the table. Of all the things I get asked about during my high school career, that's probably the one thing people talk about the most."

OHIO'S TROY VS. PIQUA FOOTBALL RIVALRY

The season-opening win over Piqua would turn out to be a high point for the Trojans in the 1969 season. Heavy on talent but light on experience, Troy would stumble to a 2-7-1 finish. Still, though, in the final game of the season against a heavily favored Wayne team, Troy found itself tied, 22–22, late in the game. On the game's final play, Conard drew up a trick play, "The West Virginia Special," a flea-flicker pass that got the ball to Walker, who was streaking down the sideline. Walker got pushed out of bounds eighteen inches short of the goal line as time expired. That offseason, Conard made his players carry around an eighteen-inch strip of white cloth to serve as a reminder of how short they had come up against Wayne.

That class of sophomores would never lose another game. Troy would finish the 1970 and 1971 seasons undefeated. The Ohio High School Athletic Association would not institute a playoff system until the following year, 1972. Still, though, the 1971 team—which outscored opponents by an average score of 41.2–5.4—is widely regarded as one of the best not only in school history but in state history as well.

That team also helped turned the tide in the rivalry. On the heels of Piqua's five-game winning streak against the Trojans, Troy would win four in a row and thirteen of the next fifteen. After beginning his career at Piqua with five straight wins over the Trojans, Asher would go 2-7 against Troy to close out his fourteen-year hall of fame career at Piqua.

Perhaps knowing his team couldn't quite stack up against the Trojans in terms of talent, Asher would spend much of the 1970s searching for any motivational edge he could find for his team. Following Troy's 54–6 victory over Piqua in 1970, a Trojan booster presented Asher with a cake inscribed with the final score in icing. Asher stored that cake in his freezer until just before the Troy-Piqua game the following season. He brought it out of storage and placed it in his team's locker room the day of the game as a reminder of the previous season's humiliation.

Conard, meanwhile, was cooking up a little gamesmanship of his own. That year, rather than bring his team to Piqua's field to warm up, he had the Trojans warm up at Troy Memorial Stadium and then loaded his players onto the bus, which arrived at the stadium just seconds before kickoff.

"All that summer, I'd driven to Piqua every way imaginable in my car," Conard said. "From that, I figured it took eight minutes to get there from Troy."

By the time Troy did arrive at the city limits, Piqua fans were waiting for them. "By the time we got off the bus, it was covered in eggs and tomatoes," Troy linebacker Tim Pierce said. "They were waiting for us at the edge of town. They absolutely covered our bus, throwing things at us. But by the time we got off the bus, we were fired up and ready to play. We came storming off that bus…I don't think anything could have stopped us that night."

Pierce was right. Once the motivational tactics had settled, the game would eventually be decided on the field—and Troy had little trouble posting its second blowout victory in a row, 36–6.

After just three years, Conard retired as Troy's coach, turning the reins over to Barry Blackstone, who continued the Trojans' domination over the Indians. In his six years as Troy coach, Blackstone went 4-2 against the Indians.

In 1973, however, Asher proved he could still come up with a game plan to defeat the Trojans.

1973: Piqua 12, Troy 7

The 1973 game between the Indians and Trojans would serve as a last hurrah of sorts for Asher. It would be his penultimate win over a Troy team and his final win over a Troy team with a winning record.

"We were sky-high for this game," Asher said in an interview with the *Troy Daily News* after the win, which snapped a four-game Troy winning streak over its rival. "The kids really wanted this one."

And thanks in large part to some key Trojan miscues, they were able to get just that.

Early in the game, Troy's defense forced a Piqua punt. On the punt, however, Troy was called for holding, giving the Indians back the ball.

"To me, that was the most important part of the game," Blackstone said in a *TDN* interview after the game. "We stopped them cold, but the penalty allowed them to keep moving and then they got some momentum. If we could have started our offense right then, we might have gotten something going. As it was, we never did in the first half."

Piqua wouldn't score on that drive but was able to switch field position and gain early momentum. After giving the ball back to Troy, the Trojan offense went nowhere, and Troy was forced to punt from deep in its own territory. On the very next play, Indian junior quarterback Bill Westfall hooked up with receiver Brent Burns on a thirty-three-yard strike.

Troy would almost tie the score on its next possession, but a long run by tailback John Mumma after a backward pass by quarterback Kevin Grump was called back on a clipping penalty. Troy would struggle to move the ball against Piqua's defense the rest of the first half, while the mistakes continued.

A Troy fumble gave Piqua back the ball. A pass interference call helped keep the Piqua drive alive, allowing Westfall to hook up with Bill Smith on a nine-yard touchdown pass, which would prove to be the game winner.

"Our biggest concern was finding a quarterback this year," Asher said. "But Bill proved tonight that he can handle the job. He had a great game."

Piqua's defense would keep Troy in check much of the rest of the night. Troy's offense didn't get on track until there was five minutes and eighteen seconds left to play in the game. Troy put together its lone scoring drive when Grump started hitting his passes to tight end Kevin Blizman and flanker John Summers. Troy capped off its lone scoring drive with a ten-yard touchdown pass from Grump to Blizman.

After receiving the ensuing kickoff, however, Piqua ran out all but the final thirty-one seconds of the game. Troy got the ball back with no timeouts at its own thirty-one, but by then it was too little, too late. Piqua was able to hold on for the victory.

"It's a great win for our kids," Asher said. "I'm happy for them."

It would be one of the final moments of happiness Piqua would see in the rivalry for a long time. Troy would win the following year, 34–6. The next year, Piqua would win, 9–0. Troy would win the next six games in a row, easily outdistancing the Indians in all six games; the closest contest in that time frame was a 16–6 Trojan victory in 1977. Between 1969 and 1977, Troy had just one losing season, a 4-6 record in 1975.

By the end of the 1970s and the early 1980s, however, both programs were in the midst of lean years. Following Asher's retirement after the 1977 season, Piqua had just one winning season from 1978 to 1985. During that same stretch, Troy had just two winning seasons.

Things were about to change for both programs, however. One man was about to arrive at each school. Those two men would forever change the rivalry, ushering in the era's "Golden Age."

Chapter 5
TROY AND PIQUA, BACK ON TOP

1984–1991

Growing up in western Pennsylvania—and then beginning his high school coaching career just across the border at Conneaut High School in northeast Ohio—Steve Nolan knew little about the Troy-Piqua rivalry.

"Honestly? I had never even heard of the cities of Troy or Piqua," Nolan said. "I didn't know anything about the teams, the high schools or the rivalry. But in the winter of 1984, a committee at Troy was looking for a coach. They had sent me a packet that included a picture of the stadium. It was one of the best high school facilities I had ever seen. Honestly, that's what convinced me that maybe I should look into this further. That was really the first time I had heard of Troy or Piqua."

Nolan accepted the head coaching position at Troy that offseason—not knowing he would spend the next thirty years of his life firmly entrenched in the most prolific rivalry in Ohio high school football history.

In 1984, both Troy and Piqua made coaching changes that would pump new life into storied programs that had hit a slump. Troy hired Nolan, who would spend the next twenty-eight years coaching there. That same year, Piqua hired Steve Magoteaux, who would spend eight years coaching at Piqua before becoming the school's athletic director and turning the reins over to assistant coach Bill Nees, who has coached the program for the past twenty-three years.

In the six years prior to Nolan's hiring, the Trojans had produced just two winning seasons, going 5-4-1 in both 1980 and 1981. In the two years before Nolan's arrival, the Trojans had gone a combined 4-15-1, including 0-10 in

OHIO'S TROY VS. PIQUA FOOTBALL RIVALRY

1982. Piqua found itself in a similar situation prior to hiring Magoteaux. In the eight years prior to Magoteaux coming to Piqua, the Indians had a winning record just once, going 6-4 in 1982. Included in that stretch were a 1-9 season in 1978 and a 0-10 record the following year. All of those struggles were unacceptable by both programs' standards.

But all of that was quickly about to change.

While Piqua's turnaround would take a few years under Magoteaux, Troy's fortunes would change immediately under Nolan.

"The first thing I noticed when we got here was how poor the strength and conditioning program had become at Troy," Nolan said. "We knew we needed to change the culture around here…and that was step one in turning everything around. When we first got here, they had some free weights and a few weight machines in a room underneath the stadium that wasn't much bigger than a closet. We immediately created a real weight room and changed the strength and conditioning program."

That change off the field would produce immediate dividends on the field for the Trojans. In Troy's first year under Nolan, the Trojans went 8-2, including a 27–18 win over Piqua in the first meeting between Nolan and Magoteaux.

In fact, so immediate and absolute was Nolan's impact on the program that he would not have a losing season at Troy during his first sixteen years there, until the Trojans went 4-6 in 1999. Dipping into a deep talent pool that was there when he arrived—but had largely underachieved prior to his arrival—Nolan led his teams to the playoffs in three of his first five seasons.

Magoteaux wouldn't experience quite the same amount of immediate success as his counterpart at Troy. The Indians went 4-5-1 his first year at the helm and 3-7 his second year coaching. While his teams struggled the first two years overall, however, Magoteaux—who came to Piqua from nearby Milton-Union—did pump new life into the rivalry from day one. While his teams lost in their first three matchups against the Trojans, all were closely contested.

Although Troy was rolling and Piqua was struggling those first three years, it became obvious that the Indians were headed in the right direction—and no matter the odds, they would be ready to give the Trojans their best shot.

Never was that more obvious than in 1985, when the two teams met for the 100th time.

THE BATTLE ON THE MIAMI

1985: Troy 26, Piqua 17

When it comes to rivalry games, the phrase "throw out the records" has become something of a cliché; some would even argue it has become overused and trite. Coaches in rivalry games love to invoke the phrase. Heavily favored coaches use it in an effort to make sure their team doesn't get complacent, while underdog coaches use it to give their teams extra motivation. Every so often, however, the words ring true.

Such was the case in 1985, when a heavily favored—and undefeated—Troy team rolled into Piqua's Wertz Stadium to take on Piqua in the 100th meeting between the two schools.

In Nolan's second year at Troy, the Trojans already had built themselves into a state-ranked powerhouse. The 1985 team was loaded with future Division I college players: senior Aaron Johnson (who would go to the Naval Academy) at quarterback, senior Kevin Mescher (Stanford) at tight end/outside linebacker, junior Mike Delwiche (Boston

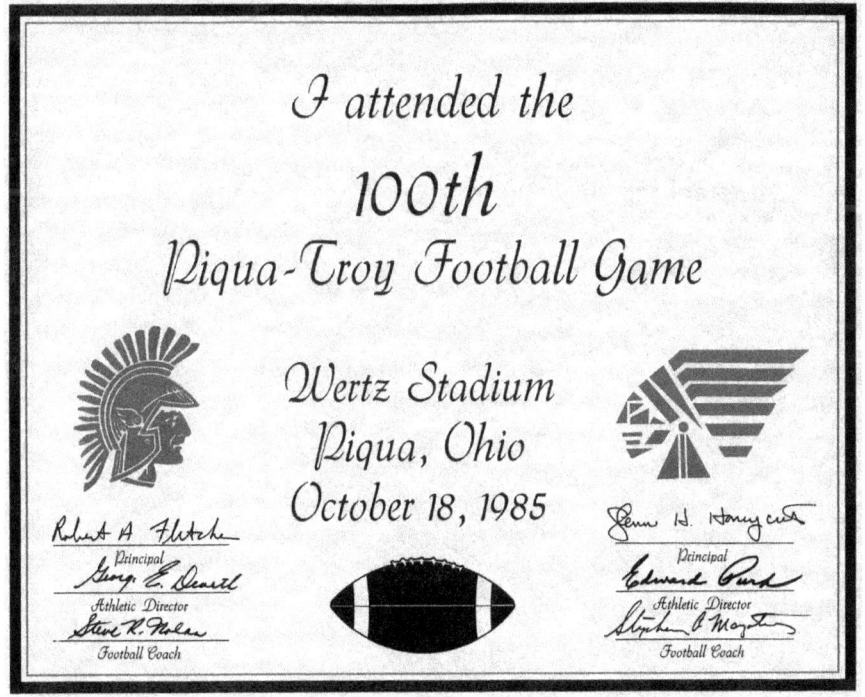

Fans who attended the 100th meeting between the two teams in 1985 received a certificate. *Courtesy of Paul Delwiche/Troy High School.*

College) at halfback and junior Mike Lohrer (North Carolina) along the offensive line.

Going into the eighth game of the season, the Trojans had steamrolled every team they had faced up to that point. Troy was averaging 46.7 points and 413 yards in total offense per game while allowing 12.3 points per game—and had allowed only two touchdowns in the first half of its previous seven games, meaning most of the points Troy had given up that season had come long after the starters on defense had retreated to the bench in the midst of blowout victories. Just the week before the Troy-Piqua game, the Trojans had blown out Vandalia-Butler 52–14 in a battle of the top two teams in the Greater Miami Valley Conference (GMVC).

Along the way, Troy's fan base—which was starving for a winner at that point—had taken up support of the team. That season, Troy's Friday night football games had again become more than just a high school athletic contest; they had become an event where one could see and be seen. Local stores couldn't keep Delwiche's no. 33 replica jersey on their shelves.

An inexperienced Piqua team, meanwhile, limped into the game with a 1-6 record. The Indians had struggled through the first half of the season with all new faces along the offensive line and didn't figure to give the Trojans much of a game—on paper at least.

Despite the fact that the Trojans were heavily favored in the game, it was the 100th meeting between the two schools—the first time two Ohio high school rivals had ever reached that mark—and anticipation in both communities was at a fever pitch.

The *Miami Valley Sunday News* had purchased one thousand plastic footballs—five hundred red footballs for Troy, five hundred blue footballs for Piqua—that cheerleaders from both schools would throw into the stands during the game. All fans who passed through the turnstiles at the 100th meeting between the two schools would receive a commemorative certificate declaring their attendance at the game.

With a standing room–only crowd ringing the cinder track around the field at Wertz Stadium, Piqua put on a show for the ages—and Troy found itself lucky to escape with the victory.

"It was insane," Nolan said. "I had never seen anything like it before in my coaching career. We probably should have blown them out, based on the talent they had that season and the talent we had that season. That was one of the best teams I had in twenty-eight years at Troy—maybe the best team. But the Piqua kids just kept coming at us and coming at us.

THE BATTLE ON THE MIAMI

"I remember they had a kid named John Apple, who played on the line. He was like a man possessed out there. He just kept crushing us play after play. No matter what we tried to do, we couldn't stop the guy. He kept blowing up everything we tried to do that night. Really, their whole team played like that."

Troy got on the board first on its opening possession on a thirty-six-yard run by Todd Canter in the first quarter. Todd Cruse added the extra point to give the Trojans a 7–0 lead. For the rest of the half, however, Piqua's defense stymied the Trojan offense, while the Indian offense kept the ball away from the Trojans until halftime.

Following Troy's first touchdown, the Trojans touched the ball only three more times during the first half. Two of those drives ended in failed fourth-down conversion attempts, while the fourth ended in a fumble.

"We didn't have the ball much," Nolan said in an interview with the *Troy Daily News* following the game. "They were keeping the ball so well we just couldn't get on the field. Our kids asked me at halftime why things weren't working. I told them it was because we didn't have the ball."

A muffed punt by the Trojans helped set up the Indians' first scoring drive. After Piqua's Steve Lord and Matt Lavy fell on the loose ball at the Troy eleven-yard line, the Piqua offense took over. Quarterback Steve Butsch—who would go on to win a state title in the pole vault while at Piqua—hooked up with Keith Keller for a ten-yard gain. That set up a one-yard touchdown plunge by Jonathan Clemons, son of former Piqua All-American Craig Clemons. Jeff Lyman kicked the extra point to tie the game. The score remained knotted at 7–7 heading into halftime.

Troy fumbled the ball to open the second half. Piqua's Chad Funderburg returned the ball to the Trojan twenty-two. Butsch moved the Indians to the Trojan four-yard line, but Trojan linebacker Dirk Naegele stopped him for a loss on third down, forcing the Indians to punt. Lyman knocked a twenty-two-yarder through the uprights, giving Piqua a 10–7 lead. It was the first time the Trojans had trailed all season.

"When we fumbled, it was really a big break for us that we held them to three points," Delwiche said after the game. "We were playing just like we had practiced all week. We weren't concentrating."

Perhaps because they were trailing for the first time all season, a fire was lit under the Trojans, who responded on the very next drive, going seventy-eight yards in twelve plays for the go-ahead touchdown. Troy never faced a third down the entire drive, with Canter and Delwiche picking up sizable gains every time they ran the ball. The drive ended with a one-yard scoring run by bullish fullback Larry Giangulio. Piqua blocked the extra point attempt, leaving the Trojans with a shaky 13–10 lead.

Piqua, as it had all night, responded immediately, driving to the Trojan thirty-one, but the Trojan defense stiffened, stopping Clemons on a running play on fourth-and-three. Troy ended the third quarter at its own forty-six.

Johnson struck quickly to open the fourth quarter, hooking up with Jesse Olden for a thirty-one-yard gain. On the very next play, Canter ran it in from nineteen yards out, extending Troy's lead to 19–10.

At that point, many 1-6 teams would have folded—not Piqua; not that night; not that rivalry.

The Indians scored on the ensuing drive, using twelve plays to go seventy-nine yards for a touchdown. Facing second-and-twenty-nine at the Indian fifteen, Butsch hooked up with Dane Widney for twenty-six yards and Charles Rose for twelve yards on consecutive plays to keep the drive alive. With four minutes and twenty-four seconds left to play in the game, Butsch hit Widney on an eight-yard pass for a touchdown, cutting the Trojans' lead to 19–17.

Troy got the ball back, and facing fourth-and-inches at the Troy twenty-four with two minutes and forty-eight seconds left to play, Nolan made a call that would help define his role in the rivalry for years to come. Deep in his own territory, he went for it.

"I think we were on the edge," Nolan said. "Too many bad things can happen on a punt. Besides, we haven't punted that much."

Johnson kept the ball on a quarterback sweep, rolled out of the arms of a Piqua defender and picked up three yards for a first down. Had he not picked up the first down, Piqua would have had the ball within range of a game-winning field goal with less than two minutes to play.

"I'll never forget that play," Johnson said. "As soon as I rolled out, I got hit right in the knees. I was able to keep my balance and keep moving. The only thing I was thinking at the time was, 'If I don't pick up this first down, we are going to lose this game.' I had no doubts then and I have no doubts now that if we didn't get that first down, they were going to win. It was a heck of a call by Coach Nolan. It took a lot of guts on his part."

Magoteaux agreed with Johnson's assessment. "It was a gutsy call," he said in an interview after the game. "I don't know if he had a choice. If he had punted, we would have gotten the ball around our 40 or so with a lot of time left."

Three plays after Johnson's first down, Delwiche—who would finish the season with more than 1,600 rushing yards but had been largely bottled up by the Piqua defense up to that point—broke loose on a 56-yard jaunt up the left sideline for a touchdown that finally iced the game for the Trojans.

"I felt we had a real good chance all the way to the final touchdown," Magoteaux said.

The 1985 game—the 100th meeting between the two teams—would have positive effects for both teams.

Troy used the momentum from that contest to finish out the regular season undefeated. It also may have learned a little something about itself while playing in its first close game of the season. The following week, Troy took on Northmont with a GMVC title on the line. Troy again found itself in a dogfight and trailed late in the game.

Perhaps using what it had learned the week prior, Troy didn't panic, despite being down late in the game. With the ball near midfield, Johnson converted a fourth down with a long pass to Mescher, who went airborne and made an acrobatic catch to keep the scoring drive alive. Troy held on for a 21–15 victory.

That win would help wrap up Troy's first undefeated regular season since 1971 and the first playoff berth in school history. The Trojans would win their first two playoff games, beating Toledo Central Catholic 36–0 in the regional semifinals and Westerville North 23–0 in the regional title game. The win against Westerville North earned the Trojans a trip to the Division I state semifinals, something that has not happened before or since. Against nationally ranked Cincinnati Moeller—which featured a kickoff return man, Ken Griffey Jr., who would go on to greater fame in a different sport—Troy's season came to an end with a 21–10 loss in a game that wasn't decided until the Crusaders scored a touchdown in the game's final minutes.

Piqua, meanwhile, also seemed to benefit from the 100th contest with its rival, even though it did end in a heartbreaking loss for the Indians. Piqua would rebound to win its final two games of the season. The next year, the Indians posted their second winning record in a decade, going 6-4. That year, Troy—which would make its second consecutive playoff appearance—squeaked by the Indians, 28–14.

In 1987, Piqua would continue to improve, going 8-2 and beating Troy 24–15, the Indians' first win over the Trojans in four years. The Indians would go 7-3 in 1988 but suffer a 39–6 loss to the Trojans. Piqua would slip slightly in 1989, going 5-5 and losing to yet another Troy playoff team, 17–14.

By 1990, however, Piqua was ready to emerge as not only one of the top local teams in the area but a state power as well. That year, with All-GMVC

OHIO'S TROY VS. PIQUA FOOTBALL RIVALRY

Troy and Piqua battle in 1988. *Courtesy of Paul Delwiche/Troy High School.*

performers Charles Lee, Chris Lyman, Tony Lyons, Ken Magoteaux, Sean Mitchell, Ethan Neuenschwander and Troy Ouhl leading the way, the Indians would go 11-2, earn the first playoff berth in school history and reach the Division I state semifinals.

Piqua would defeat Troy 20–7 during the regular season and then roll through the first two rounds of the playoffs, beating Grove City 3–0 and Columbus Brookhaven 34–7. Cincinnati Princeton would end Piqua's run with a 34–7 victory over the Indians in the state semifinals.

The following year, 1991, it was more of the same for the Indians. With much of the same talent returning from the previous year, the Indians finished the regular season 10-0—their first perfect regular season since 1947. Included in those regular season wins was a 24–6 victory over Troy, one of only two losses for the Trojans that season. In the first round of the playoffs that year, Piqua defeated Grove City 14–7 in the regional semifinals but lost to Brookhaven, 14–3, in the regional championship game.

That would be Magoteaux's final year leading the Indians, as he took over as the school's athletic director in 1992. In his relatively brief run as head coach, however, his value to the program cannot be understated. He instilled discipline in his players and brought a winning culture back to the program—something that had been sorely missing since Coach Asher's departure in the 1970s. He turned the program around—and it would remain that way long after his last game on the sidelines.

In addition to changing the culture at Piqua, Magoteaux would leave two lasting legacies that would continue long after his departure. The first was genetic: his sons Ken, Bryan and Kyle all went on to become star players for the Indians. The second was a human resources decision. In 1985, Magoteaux brought in Bill Nees as his assistant coach. In 1992, Nees—after stints as the offensive/defensive line coach and defensive coordinator at Piqua—became head coach following Magoteaux's ascension to the program's athletic director.

Magoteaux's prescient hiring choice would help set up two decades of Nolan vs. Nees—and what many who follow the rivalry closely have come to refer to as the "Golden Age of Troy vs. Piqua."

Chapter 6

NOLAN VS. NEES

Sometimes, seemingly equal but opposite forces come together at the same time, and the results often are magical.

Muhammad Ali and Joe Frazier set the boxing world afire in the 1970s with their epic fight trilogy. Incredible talents individually, they were even better when paired off against each other. Soon after, basketball legends Magic Johnson and Larry Bird both reached the height of their powers at the exact same time, first squaring off in the NCAA championship game in 1979 and then battling for better than a decade in the NBA finals. Certainly, Johnson and Bird, had they played in separate eras, still would have been superstars. Their talents were undeniable. But the fact that they squared off against each other, year after year and season after season, made the intrigue all the more palpable. They made each other better.

Troy's Steve Nolan and Piqua's Bill Nees are the greatest coaches in their respective schools' histories. Nolan, coach at Troy from 1984 to 2012, is by far the winningest coach in Troy history. Nees, an assistant at Piqua High School from 1985 to 1991 and the head coach from 1992 to the present, is the winningest coach in Piqua history. Individually, their legacies are secure.

Together, their legacies are the stuff of lore. And with their handprints all over some of the greatest games in the history of the Troy-Piqua rivalry, it's hard to imagine them not going down in history together.

"I think, for an entire generation of fans of the rivalry, it's hard to remember a time when Bill Nees didn't coach at Piqua and when Steve Nolan didn't coach at Troy," said former Piqua player Matt Finkes, who played under

THE BATTLE ON THE MIAMI

Nees at Piqua before going on to become an All-American defensive end at The Ohio State University. "There's so much longevity there on both sides. Nolan was at Troy forever, and Nees has been at Piqua forever.

"Both have been successful at each school, too. I think you would have to say each has had a huge impact on the rivalry. As a Piqua player, I knew it meant something special when you beat a Steve Nolan–coached team because you knew they were going to be well coached and they were going to give you their best shot. I'm sure guys who played at Troy would say the same thing—it meant something special when you were able to beat a Bill Nees–coached team. That's just the way it was for more than twenty years."

Both began their football careers as ultra-successful players at their respective high schools and would attain success at every level before their individual paths brought them to Ohio's most prolific high school football rivalry.

Troy coach Steve Nolan in 2011. *Courtesy of Lee Woolery/Speedshot Photo.*

Nolan began his football career as a running back at General McLane High School in western Pennsylvania. Although undersized, he possessed power, speed and a grim determination that would allow him to earn all-state honors. He would go on to earn all-conference honors at Clarion University.

Following his graduation from college, he took several positions as an assistant college football coach before realizing his heart was at the high school level. He moved on to Conneaut High School in northeast Ohio, where he led his team to several conference championships before accepting the head coaching job at Troy.

Nees grew up on what he jokingly refers to as "the mean streets of Lima, Ohio," playing along the offensive and defensive lines at Lima Central Catholic High School. Following his graduation from high school, he went on to play offensive guard at Baldwin-Wallace University in Berea, Ohio, where he helped lead the team to an Amos Alonzo Stagg Bowl victory and a Division III national championship in 1978.

Following his graduation from college, Nees received a tryout with the Montreal Alouettes of the Canadian Football League. After being cut by the team in his first training camp, he accepted an assistant coaching position at Graham High School in Saint Paris, Ohio. He spent two years as an assistant at Graham before accepting an assistant coaching position at nearby Piqua. In 1987, Nees was promoted from offensive and defensive line coach to defensive coordinator. In 1992, he was named head coach when then head coach Steve Magoteaux became the school's athletic director.

Nees's arrival as an assistant at Piqua coincided directly with Nolan's second—and most successful—season as Troy's head coach. The two would spend the next twenty-seven years linked together, producing some of the most epic battles in rivalry history.

Nolan says he knew right away that Nees would be a worthy adversary. "You could tell right away he was going to be successful—and it would only be a matter of time before he became a head coach," Nolan said. "Although it was only my second year here at Troy, you could see right away the impact he would have on their defense as an assistant. Then when he became head coach, we knew we were going to be in for some battles.

"You always knew that every time you faced a Bill Nees team, they were going to be well coached. And his teams were always going to be prepared. As a coach, you had better be willing to put in the extra work in practice and watching film to prepare for the game because you knew Bill Nees was going to be doing the same. You had to be willing to put in the same amount of work as him. He works as hard or harder than any coach I've ever known."

Nees, too, knew immediately he would have his hands full with Nolan. "Steve Nolan is a great coach," Nees said. "His teams are well prepared every time you play them. And it always seemed like he had something special for us every time we played. You knew you could count on them to do certain things, but he also had a way of maybe sneaking in a few things. Sometimes he would pull out something you hadn't seen him do in fifteen years for the Troy-Piqua game…and it usually worked."

As is the case with so many rivalries, contrasting styles made the matchups all the more intriguing.

THE BATTLE ON THE MIAMI

During his stay at Troy, Nolan became known for producing stellar running backs and pinball-like numbers on offense. In his twenty-eight years at Troy, Nolan churned out twenty-six 1,000-yard rushers, the most noteworthy of whom was Ryan Brewer, who would set a state record in 1998 by rushing for 2,856 yards in just ten games. Brewer would win the coveted Mr. Football Ohio award that year.

In his beloved, run-heavy wing-t offense, Troy would routinely produce eye-popping numbers running the ball on offense. "Just look at his track record," Brewer said of Nolan. "Look at how many great running backs he has produced during his career. Even when teams knew what was coming, they had a hard time stopping the run. When he was coaching, you knew Troy was going to line up and run the ball right at you…good luck stopping it."

Nees, meanwhile, became known for producing stellar defenses and, in particular, defensive linemen who had Division I college coaches lining up outside his office. During his time at Piqua, Nees coached two future All-Americans in Finkes (who was an All-American at Ohio State in 1993) and Quinn Pitcock (a defensive end who was an All-American at Ohio State in 2007). He also coached blue chip prospect Antwon Jones, who went on to play at the University of Notre Dame.

"Playing at Piqua, especially under Bill Nees, helped my career greatly," Finkes said. "From a technique aspect, I learned to play with my hands and not my shoulder pads. Honestly, Bill Nees was at the forefront of teaching that. When I first started in high school, the forearm shiver was still being taught and used as a block-shedding technique in high school.

"Bill Nees taught his defensive linemen that they couldn't just rely on going out and using your physical tools to go out and overpower somebody. The higher you go up the food chain in football, the more equal everybody becomes and the less that works. You have to be able to play with your hands, and you have to have good technique. I got thrust into that situation right away at Ohio State. When you are eating every day and trying to stay at 250 pounds, you aren't going to be able to go out and overpower Korey Stringer or Orlando Pace in practice. You have to have good technique."

Not that either coach was a one-trick pony, mind you. Nolan coached some stellar defenses and produced a number of talented players on defense, most notably outside linebacker Jason Manson, the Division I Co-Defensive Player of the Year in the state of Ohio in 1996, who went on to play at the University of Toledo. And Nees has coached his fair share of great offenses and offensive talents, including Brandon Saine, the electric running back who was named Mr. Football Ohio in 2006 while leading the Indians to a

Division II state championship. Saine would go on to play running back at The Ohio State University.

Still, though, they cemented their legacies within the rivalry as Nolan's offense vs. Nees's defense. The irresistible object vs. the immovable force.

Aside from that major difference, however, the two shared many of the same qualities. From their mustachioed visages to their unquestioned coaching leadership, they had plenty in common. Both attained high levels of success. Both had gruff public exteriors but dry senses of humor that would frequently have their assistant coaches and players rolling on the floor with laughter. Both were strict disciples of their strength and conditioning programs.

In their head-to-head meetings, Nolan held a slim edge against Nees, with his teams going 13-9 against the Indians, thanks in large part to a five-game winning streak to close out his career at Troy. Nees, meanwhile, had greater success in the postseason, taking two teams to the Division II state championship game in 2000 and 2006 and winning a state championship in 2006, the only state title either school has won since the Ohio High School Athletic Association instituted a playoff system in 1972.

During their coaching careers, Nolan and Nees would wage numerous memorable battles. Nees's Indians scored on the final play of the game in 1993 to defeat a heavily favored Troy team. Nolan's Trojans won the only overtime meeting between the two schools in 1995. Troy blew out Piqua in 1996, only to see the Indians return the favor in 2006. Troy won an epic battle between the two schools in 2007 by scoring in the game's final minutes.

As incredible as all those years were, however, most still point to the first two meetings—yes, meetings plural—between the two coaches in 1992 as perhaps the most remarkable season in the history of the Troy-Piqua rivalry. That year, Troy and Piqua would battle twice—and two communities nearly imploded under the pressure and magnitude of the rivalry.

Chapter 7
THE GAMES OF THE CENTURY

1992

In a ninety-three-year rivalry filled with several "Game of the Century" matchups, this was supposed to be the big one. In nearly a century of grudge matches filled with moments and memories, with passion and perspiration, the 1992 battle between Troy and Piqua featured two teams reaching their apex at the exact same time. It was two rival teams rolling toward the new millennium, about to play in the biggest game of them all. It had two coaches who would eventually become legends at their schools and two teams loaded with talent. The eyes of the state would be on Miami County as a pair of state-ranked teams squared off in a game that was bigger than Christmas, a lifetime of birthdays and the Fourth of July all rolled into one. One game to determine who was the rightful heir to the throne.

What no one knew at the time, however, was that it was a battle so nice, they had to do it twice. Seven weeks later, the two teams would meet again in the Division I playoffs.

In the fall of 1992, in the fifth week of the season, Troy and Piqua met up at Troy Memorial Stadium in a game that exceeded the hype and expectation of the 106 previous battles. Piqua came into the game 5-0 and ranked no. 6 in the state of Ohio. Troy also came into the game undefeated and ranked no. 10 in the state.

T-shirts were made. Numerous pep rallies were held. Media outlets were dispatched as television news helicopters filled the air. If anyone wanted to rob a house in Troy or Piqua, that would have been the night to do it, as seemingly everyone from both towns was at the game.

OHIO'S TROY VS. PIQUA FOOTBALL RIVALRY

"I think it was a matter of two great teams reaching their height at the exact same time," Troy coach Steve Nolan said. "They had been to the playoffs the previous two years, so I think everyone kind of knew what to expect from them. I think we were probably a little more of a surprise, but that probably made our fans a little more excited for the game, to be honest with you. They had handled us pretty well the past two years, so I think we definitely took on more of an underdog role. But that just seemed to get our fans a little more excited about the game."

"It was the kind of game players and coaches both dream of participating in," said Piqua coach Bill Nees, who would be on the sidelines for the first time as a head coach in the rivalry. "The rivalry is always a big deal anyway, but now you had the added bonus of both teams being undefeated and state-ranked, which was pretty unusual. It was a pretty big deal for both communities, obviously. At the time, that was the game everyone was looking forward to. I don't think anyone was looking ahead to a possible rematch in the playoffs. Sure, it was a possibility, but you wanted to win the first one, just in case there wasn't going to be a rematch."

Troy came into the season as a relative unknown quantity. Sure, Troy had gone 8-2 the previous season and returned most of its skill position players on offense—senior Mark Evilsizor at quarterback, senior Chad Dillow at halfback and juniors Brad Clay and Scot Brewer at fullback and halfback, respectively—but the team faced serious questions along the offensive line. Troy had four new starters along the offensive line, including a pair of five-foot, eight-inch, 180-pound junior guards in Shane Fobian and Bill Garfield, two players so small Nolan nicknamed them "The Weebles" after a popular 1970s child's toy—as in, "The Weebles may wobble, but they don't fall down."

Although it did have a new head coach, Piqua entered the season with far fewer question marks. The Indians had been to the playoffs each of the two previous seasons, including a state semifinals appearance in 1990. They were battle-tested, featuring twenty-five seniors on their roster. The team was loaded with stars, none bigger than defensive tackle Matt Finkes, who would go on to become an All-American defensive end at The Ohio State University. Offensively, the Indians were led by senior quarterback Ken Magoteaux, a three-year starter and the son of former coach Steve Magoteaux.

It didn't take long for Troy to erase some of the doubts about its offensive line in 1992. In the season opener, the Trojans rolled to a 78–20 victory over Springfield South, piling up 720 total rushing yards and flirting with the national high school record. In week two, however, the Trojans were tested by Wayne. Troy trailed early and needed a comeback to pull out a 29–23 victory. From there, the Trojans were nearly unstoppable in the next two games, pounding Toledo Libby 61–0 and Vandalia-Butler 32–6.

Piqua faced a similar route to "The Game." Like the Trojans, the Indians had a relatively easy time in the opener, defeating Springfield North 42–18, but were tested in the second game. Against Fairmont, Piqua got out to an early 21–6 lead but would need to hold on for the win. The game was not decided until linebacker Eric Lavey intercepted a 2-point conversion attempt with no time left on the clock. With that game perhaps serving as a wake-up call, the Indians were able to cruise to wins in the next two games, rolling Urbana 35–7 and defeating Greenville 34–20.

And so, midway through the regular season, the stage was set. It was two storied programs, both with rabid fan bases, meeting in a clash of undefeated, state-ranked teams. It was all that anyone could possibly have hoped for.

Well, for the first time, anyway.

Part I: Troy 22, Piqua 7

Given the perfect storm of factors going into the game, the early October matchup between the two teams became the ultimate high school sports spectacle, and both communities nearly buckled under the weight of the hype.

In the week leading up to the Friday night showdown, both cities held multiple pep rallies and public appearances by players and coaches. Hundreds of T-shirts commemorating the game were sold at both high schools. Red ribbons festooned the lampposts along the city streets of Troy, while blue ribbons were wrapped around every available streetlight in Piqua.

The game was moved from the sports pages to the front pages in both communities. More than a dozen press credentials were issued for the game, as three local newspapers, two radio stations, a local cable access station and all three local television news stations wanted in on the action. On the night of the game, television news helicopters filled the air.

Thousands of fans lined up hours before kickoff, hoping to get the best seat available in Troy's normally spacious stadium.

It had reached the point where the game itself almost seemed secondary.

"I expected it, but…emotionally, it just nearly engulfed you," Troy defensive tackle Joe Williams said in an interview with the *Troy Daily News*.

OHIO'S TROY VS. PIQUA FOOTBALL RIVALRY

When both teams walked out onto the field for warm-ups, they were met with a thunderous response from the crowd. By the time the team captains met at midfield for the coin toss, fans were at a fever pitch.

"It was pure adrenaline," Troy linebacker Rob Shook told the *Troy Daily News* after the game. "We had the stereo in the lockerroom cranked up, and then went out on the field and everyone went crazy. Walking out on the field in front of a crowd like that gave you chills."

Although thrilling, both teams seemed to wilt early under the intense pressure of playing in front of so many sets of eyes.

Troy took the opening kickoff and drove to the Indian thirty-eight, but the drive stalled and the Trojans were forced to punt. The punt rolled dead at the Piqua three-yard line, but the Indians were able to put together a drive of their own, marching down to the Trojan fifteen. On second down, however, a Troy defensive back picked off a Magoteaux pass deep in Trojan territory. It would be one of six interceptions the Trojans had on the night, including two by Alex Shilt.

Troy again started driving the ball behind the three-headed monster of Dillow, Clay and Brewer in the backfield. Again, however, turnovers played a key role as Evilsizor fumbled at the Piqua twenty-nine, thwarting another scoring drive.

Two plays later, however, Troy picked off its second pass of the night as defensive back Tom Barr stepped in front of another Magoteaux pass at the Piqua twenty-eight.

"They thought the run-and-shoot worked, but it didn't," Barr said in an interview following the game. "I knew I had to play my best game and the secondary knew they had to play the best games of their lives."

After Troy's second interception of the night, however, the Trojans offered up their second fumble of the game, which Brian Shepard pounced on for his second fumble recovery of the night. Midway through the first quarter, both teams already had turned the ball over twice. Piqua drove to the Trojan thirty-eight, but yet another drive stalled, and the Indians were forced to punt.

Early in the second quarter, finally, one team was able to put together a scoring drive without losing its grip on the ball. Troy went eighty yards following the punt, with Evilsizor sneaking in from a yard out for a touchdown and Shook booting the extra point as the Trojans drew first blood, 7–0.

"I definitely think the crowd and the atmosphere had an effect on both teams," Nolan said. "How could it not? You are talking about high school kids playing in front of a crowd two or three times the size of what some small colleges see on a weekly basis. Plus you had all of the hype leading up

THE BATTLE ON THE MIAMI

to the week of the game. I don't know of any high school kid that wouldn't have been nervous going into that game."

Troy's lead would be short-lived, however, as Piqua—perhaps because of all the interceptions that had been thrown up until that point—eschewed the passing game to close out the half and inserted its "heavy package" in the backfield, with Finkes, Ryan Beougher and Scott Buecker all carrying the ball on the ensuing drive.

Piqua pounded out sixty-six yards—aided by a long pass from Magoteaux to Brooks Dodson—on the next drive, with the six-foot, four-inch, 245-pound Finkes bulling his way into the end zone from a yard out. Ryan Hulme booted the extra point, and the two teams went into halftime of the true "Game of the Century" knotted at 7–7.

Piqua took the opening kickoff of the second half and drove to the Trojan twenty-eight, but Shook went airborne to block a forty-five-yard field goal attempt by Hulme, giving the Trojans the ball back. Troy drove to the Indian one-yard line, but Evilsizor fumbled the snap and Buecker fell on it, giving the Indians the ball back with ninety-nine yards of field in front of them.

That may have been a fortuitous bounce for the Trojans, however. On the very next play, Williams trapped Finkes in the backfield, giving the Trojans a 9–7 lead.

"I guess that is my claim to fame," Williams would say years afterward. "Obviously you have someone like Finkes who went on to play at Ohio State. I was never really tall enough to play college football at the next level, so I guess you could say that was the shining moment of my football career."

Troy took the free kick and smashed its way down to the Piqua four-yard line, but Shook's field goal attempt was wide left. Not that it much mattered, however, as Troy's defense would again help decide the game, again on an interception.

With four minutes left to play in the game, Dillow—who rushed for a game-high 124 yards while also playing full time at linebacker—stepped in front of a Magoteaux pass and returned it 32 yards for a touchdown to put the Trojans up 16–7.

"We owed them—owed them big time," Dillow said in a *TDN* interview after the game. "We should have beat them last year, but we didn't play with any emotion. This made up for it."

It was the final of six Trojan interceptions in the game—Magoteaux threw four, while junior Kevin Johns, a supreme talent who worked his way up the depth chart into co-quarterbacking duties with Magoteaux that season—threw two.

Magoteaux and Johns—who came into the game having completed a combined 66 of 107 passes for 714 yards—completed just 7 of 24 passes for 72 yards against the Trojans. They threw nearly as many passes to Trojan defenders—in addition to Shilt, Barr and Dillow, Scott Young and Gene Steinke also recorded interceptions—as they did their own receivers.

"I don't think we ever came into the game expecting to be intercepted six times," Nees said after the game. "We've only been intercepted once the whole year. Up to this point, the quarterbacks have done a fantastic job."

Dillow's interception return for a touchdown would turn out to be the backbreaker. Troy's defense would force a punt on the Indians' next drive and then put the nail in the coffin with a fifty-three-yard run by Clay, followed by a five-yard touchdown run by Brewer for the game's final points.

"It was a great win for the kids and for the community," Nolan said.

Little did anyone know at the time, however, that it was just the first act in a two-part passion play.

"Honestly, once we got that game behind us, we weren't really thinking about the possibility of seeing them again in the playoffs," Nolan said. "We knew it was out there, since we were in the same region, but our first goal around here is to win the league. We always figure that if we win the league, the playoffs take care of themselves. Once that first game was over, our focus went right to winning the league. The playoffs were the furthest thing from our mind at that point."

The Indians may have been a little more cognizant of a playoff rematch, but like Nolan, Nees wouldn't allow his team to look too far into the future.

"Sure, it's something we thought about…how could you not?" Nees said. "Losing a game like that, with that much emotion, you always want another chance. Most times, teams don't get that opportunity. But it's not something we could dwell on too much. If you start thinking like that, you allow yourself to get trapped. I think any time you are a coach, you always want your team's focus to be on the following week."

Ironically, after all the platitudes following the Trojans' win over the rival Indians, Troy did indeed fall flat the next week. An emotionally drained Troy team fumbled the opening kickoff and never was able to recover after that in a 14–3 loss to Northmont.

Troy did manage to right the ship the following week in a thrilling 21–20 homecoming win over Greenville and then outlasted Sidney 23–12 the following week. The Trojans closed out the regular season with blowout victories over Trotwood-Madison (36–0) and West Carrollton (54–12).

THE BATTLE ON THE MIAMI

The loss to Troy had ripple effects for the Indians. First and foremost, it forced the Indians to enter the second half of the season with a completely different mindset.

"Going into the Troy game, I think we may have thought we were a little better than we actually were," Finkes said. "We had just about everybody coming back from the year before, and I think we may have taken not only Troy lightly, but a few other teams lightly up to that point, as well. I think once we lost that first game, we finally started to realize that talent wasn't enough…we were going to have to work a lot harder than we were if we wanted to get a second chance at Troy. It was really an eye-opening experience for us."

Losing to Troy—particularly considering how the Indians lost, throwing six interceptions while allowing quarterbacks to share time—forced Piqua to reevaluate a few things schematically as well. Soon after the loss to Troy, Johns—who would go on to become a record-setting quarterback at the University of Dayton—would take over full-time duties as quarterback. Magoteaux, meanwhile, would move to running back, allowing Piqua to get two of its best athletes on the field at the same time.

Piqua would also change its philosophy, moving away from the run-and-shoot toward a more ground-oriented attack. The change in philosophy not only made the Indians more efficient on offense but also allowed their bone-crunching defense to carry more of the load.

"Sometimes, a loss isn't always a bad thing—provided you learn something from it," Nees said. "I think in that first game, Troy was able to expose some of the flaws in things we were doing. They definitely took advantage of the mistakes we made. They did some things that maybe we hadn't seen before from any of the teams we had faced up until that point. I don't think you ever want to lose a game—especially a game like that—but I definitely think you can learn from your losses. That's something the 1992 team was able to do."

Like Troy, Piqua may have been suffering from a hangover the following week but was able to hold on for a 17–14 win over an overmatched Trotwood-Madison team. The Indians followed that up with a 29–0 win over Vandalia-Butler and a 46–15 victory over Sidney.

In the final game of the season, Northmont—perhaps feeling slighted at the attention its Greater Miami Valley Conference counterparts had received all season—wrapped up a conference title by ragdolling Piqua, 21–0, in much the same way it had done to Troy four weeks prior.

Not that it much mattered in the grand scheme of things, however. Both the Trojans and Indians, by virtue of their 9-1 regular season finishes, had earned spots in the Division I regional playoffs. Troy would meet Springfield North in the opening round, while Piqua would meet Toledo St. Francis. Wins by both would set up the greatest rematch in rivalry history.

Both teams would take care of business in the regional semifinals, with Troy overcoming a slow start to defeat Springfield North 34–8 and Piqua playing lights-out defense in a 13–0 victory.

As the clock ticked down in Dayton's Welcome Stadium during the final moments of Troy's win over Springfield North, a chant went up from a small contingent of Troy fans who finally felt safe vocalizing what many had been thinking when the playoff pairings were announced: "We want Piqua! We want Piqua!"

One week later, they would get all they could possibly want—and more.

Part II: Piqua 20, Troy 7

Of the 20,000 residents living in Troy in the fall of 1992, roughly 19,999 were excited—or at the very least intrigued—about the Trojans playing in a rematch with the Indians. The lone vote of dissension was Nolan himself.

"It's tough playing a team twice in the same season—especially if your team won the first game," Nolan said. "From a psychological standpoint, if you won the first game, you really have nothing to gain by playing the same team a second team. If you beat them again, OK, you beat them the first time, so you were supposed to win. If you lose, it's like, 'What went wrong the second time?' Obviously, it's not quite that simple. You make adjustments, but so does the other team.

"If you lose the first game, I think that gives you a huge psychological edge going into the second game. You really don't have anything to lose. If you win that second game, you look like a superhero. Plus, there's the revenge factor. I think it's easier to get your team up to play a team for the second time if you lose the first game."

Needless to say, Nees was far more enthused for his team to get a second chance at the Trojans.

"I didn't want to spend the rest of my life as the answer to some sort of trivia question: 'Who is the only Piqua coach to lose to Troy in the playoffs?'" Nees said. "I think our kids were ready to play that game. The kids worked so hard the week of that game. We had cots at the high schools. The game films were burning. Most times when you lose to a team during the regular

THE BATTLE ON THE MIAMI

season, that's it. You don't get another chance at them—especially your seniors. Our kids, especially our seniors, were blessed to get that second chance. They weren't about to let that opportunity slip through their fingers a second time."

In spite of the higher stakes, there was far less hype preceding the second game. There were fewer pep rallies and public appearances for both teams, fewer T-shirts sold and, on a rainy, chilly night in Dayton at Welcome Stadium, the neutral site for the playoff game, only eight thousand fans showed up—an impressive number for a high school football game, to be sure, but barely more than half the number of fans who had shown up for the previous meeting.

As had been the case in the first meeting, defense and the ability to force turnovers would define the game, particularly early. Piqua's defense set the tone from the outset, not allowing Troy's vaunted offense to move the ball in the first half. Piqua's offense, meanwhile, didn't put many balls in the air—the Indians attempted only twelve passes all night, half the number of passes they attempted in the first game—instead going with a punishing ground game led by Magoteaux and Beougher.

"They did what I thought they should have done right away," Nolan said in an interview after the game. "They just pounded the ball right at us. And we didn't move the ball effectively in the second half, or in either half, really. There was not a whole lot to it. They just lined up across from us on the line, man-on-man. They were saying, 'We have the better athletes up front and you're going to have to beat us.' And that's what they did."

Seemingly, the lessons Piqua had learned in the first game were at play in the second.

"I think we learned our lesson from the first Troy game," Nees said. "We did our homework and we found some things we couldn't do. The way we played in the first game, we had to. We looked at the running game more. We had to establish that."

Still, though, Troy's defense matched Piqua nearly blow for blow in the first half—and actually ended up drawing first blood. Early in the second quarter, Johns dropped back to pass, pumped once and appeared ready to throw the pass in the direction of Dodson, who had broken loose from the Trojan secondary. Before he could deliver the pass, however, Trojan defensive end Randy Breedlove delivered a bone-jarring hit, shaking the ball loose. Shook picked up the ball off the turf and raced twenty-one yards for a touchdown. He also added the extra point, giving the Trojans a 7–0 lead that would stand going into halftime.

OHIO'S TROY VS. PIQUA FOOTBALL RIVALRY

Despite being down 7–0 at halftime, however, the Indians were hardly deterred. If anything, being on the short end at halftime may only have served to fuel the Indians' fire.

"As a team, we bond together at halftime," lineman Joel Cade, one of the Indians' emotional leaders, said in a *Troy Daily News* interview after the game. "We came together and did what we needed to win this game."

In fact, so fired up were the Indians in the locker room at halftime that Nees chose to throw out the halftime speech he had planned. "We went in and before I could say anything, they were screaming in my face," Nees said. "I thought, 'OK, let's go out and do it.'"

Which is exactly what the Indians would end up doing in the second half. The defense would essentially shut down the Trojan offense in the second half, not allowing a score—raising to eight the number of quarters of playoff football in which the Indians did not allow a score to an opposing offense.

"We didn't do anything different [in the second half]," Finkes said in an interview with the *Piqua Daily Call* following the game. "We tried to come off the ball harder and make the sure tackles. I think we missed a lot of tackles in the first half."

Troy's offense, which entered the game averaging better than 350 rushing yards per game, finished the game with just 195 yards on the ground and 216 yards in total offense. In the second half, Piqua's defense held Troy to a scant 54 yards in total offense. The Trojans finished the game with only nine first downs. Piqua's Dodson also recorded both an interception and a fumble recovery. His fumble recovery at the Trojan 36 in the third quarter helped spark the Piqua offense, and once the Indians got rolling on that side of the ball, the Trojans couldn't do anything to stem the tide.

Following Dodson's fumble recovery, he was on the receiving end of a fifteen-yard pass from Johns. On the very next play, Johns found Ryan Hulme all alone in the end zone for a twenty-one-yard touchdown pass. Hulme booted the extra point, tying the game.

Piqua had grabbed control of the momentum and, with its ground-churning offense, wasn't about to give it back.

The Indians stuffed the Trojans on the next drive, taking over at their own forty-one. With Beougher lined up in the backfield next to Johns on an apparent pass play, Nees was one step ahead, calling the draw to Beougher.

Beougher took the handoff into the right side of the line and then cut back toward the middle of the field. He drifted toward the left sideline and, with a pair of Trojans in hot pursuit, turned on the afterburners near the thirty and outraced Troy's last line of defense into the end zone for a fifty-one-yard, backbreaking touchdown.

"Beougher is a beast," Nees told the *Piqua Daily Call* after the game. "What can you say? You look at him on the sideline and his eyes are rolled back in his head. He is huffing and puffing. You put him in the game and he can go coast to coast. He can put that burst of energy on when he needs it."

On Troy's ensuing drive, another big play by Dodson set up the play that would ice the game. With a little more than eight minutes remaining in the game, he hauled in a tipped pass and returned it to the Piqua thirty-four.

Twelve plays later, Magoteaux bulled his way in from a yard out, giving Piqua a 20–7 lead, the eventual win and final bragging rights for a season many still look back at fondly as one of the greatest in the history of the rivalry.

"It's been like a dark cloud that's followed us around for six weeks," Nees said after the game. "How many teams are lucky enough to get a second chance and correct mistakes? We'd rather have a monkey on our backs for six weeks than do it for a whole year. The kids have worked so hard for this."

Troy's season came to an end at 10-2. Piqua would go on to play in the state semifinals for the second time in three years, falling to Cincinnati St. Xavier, 30–7. Piqua was able to stay close early—the Indians trailed just 14–7 at halftime—but the Bombers were able to make several big plays in the second half to pull away.

And truthfully, that should have ended the most storied chapter in the history of Ohio high school football's most prolific rivalry. Drop the curtain. End scene. Fade to black.

The pair of games in 1992 should have brought an end to an era. Had it been a fictional story, the two programs would have limped to the end of the century, but the memories of that season would have remained with everyone for the long haul.

As things turned out, however, 1992 wasn't the end but merely the kickoff to perhaps the most glorious decade in the history of the rivalry. While the years from 1993 to 1999 may not have been able to match the 1992 battle in terms of drama, they certainly weren't short on excitement.

Troy and Piqua were in the middle of the rivalry's "Golden Age."

Chapter 8
THE GOLDEN AGE

1990–1999

Every player who has ever participated in the Troy-Piqua rivalry—no matter on which side he played—wants his legacy to stand a little taller than those who come before him or those who will come after him. They all want to think their game was the most epic or the most dramatic. They want to forever be able to claim their rightful place in history. They want fans to look back and definitively say, "That was the greatest era in the history of a storied rivalry."

Considering the debate is purely subjective, all can make that claim. It doesn't mean, however, that all of them will be right. There can be only one true "golden era" in the history of the rivalry. Only one framed period of time lays claim to being the era that produced the most superstars, the greatest drama, the most intriguing results and, truthfully, the best overall experience for players, fans and coaches.

Although they admittedly are unbiased when it comes to the subject, both Nees and Nolan make a strong case for the decade of the 1990s being the "golden era" in the history of the rivalry.

"I think you could pretty easily look back at the 1990s and say that really was the 'Golden Age' of the rivalry," Nees said. "It seemed like that decade had a little bit of everything. You had incredibly talented players, you had teams that fared well, you had the classic playoff game. It just seemed like you had two programs, both at the height of their powers, so to speak, playing one another every year. Pick any one of those games that you want from that decade, and it seems like just about every one of them, with the odd exception here or there, was a classic."

THE BATTLE ON THE MIAMI

Nolan agreed. "It would be hard to argue against that decade, for sure," he said. "You had incredibly talented players on both sides—kids who went on to succeed at the college level and, in some cases, make it all the way to the NFL. Piqua had [Matt] Finkes and [Antwon] Jones; we had [Kris] Dielman and [Ryan] Brewer. And that was just some of the talent that played for both teams in the game. Plus, it seemed like every year it was a war. There weren't a whole lot of blowouts. No matter how good we were, we always got their best shot, and vice versa. Those were some absolute wars we played back in the 1990s. I think it was a pretty special time."

There are, of course, numbers to back up both coaches. The two teams met eleven times from 1990 to 1999, with Piqua winning six times and Troy winning five. Unlike the 1920s, 1930s and 1940s, which were dominated by Piqua, or the 1950s, 1970s and 1980s, which were dominated by Troy, neither team was able to pull far ahead of the other in the 1990s. This led to plenty of drama—and high ticket sales—for fans, who couldn't afford to miss the game. Every year, the game was in doubt.

When they weren't playing each other, both Troy and Piqua dominated their non-rivalry competition. Between the two of them, there was only one losing season the entire decade, with Troy going 4-6 in 1999. Piqua averaged 9.5 wins and 2.0 losses per season during the 1990s, while Troy wasn't far behind with an average of 8.1 and 2.5 losses per season. The Troy teams combined for ten playoff appearances during the decade, with Troy going four times and Piqua going six. In fact, from 1990 to 1999, the postseason featured either Troy or Piqua—or both—every year except 1998.

Troy and Piqua also combined to win or share the Greater Miami Valley Conference nine out of ten times during the decade. The only time neither Troy nor Piqua won the title was that magical year in 1992 when the two teams were expending all their energy battling each other, allowing another team to slip through the back door.

It was, as Nees pointed out, a decade that had "something for everyone." It even had a huge upset—and a little controversy.

1993: Piqua 16, Troy 15

It was supposed to be a year of redemption for Troy. With the taste of the previous year's loss to Piqua in the playoffs still resting heavily on their tongues, the Trojans entered the 1993 season on a mission. With all but a handful of starters returning from the 1992 playoff team, anything less than a perfect season, a trip to the playoffs and—most important—beating Piqua and gaining a measure of revenge would have been seen as a colossal disappointment.

The Indians, however, had far more question marks heading into the season. The Indians had lost twenty-five seniors—many of whom played key starting roles for Piqua.

While Troy entered the rivalry game 4-0, Piqua already had a loss on its record—just the second regular-season loss in three years for the Indians.

Not only did most expect the Trojans to win the game, but quite a few were expecting a highly motivated Troy team to blow out Piqua in Wertz Stadium.

"I think it would be safe to say most people considered Troy the favorite in that game," Nees said. "They had pretty much everyone back from the year before, while we had lost twenty-five seniors. But I don't think people realized how much talent we had coming back, too. We still had a number of kids who had the experience of playing on a state semifinal team the year before, but we also had quite a few younger kids who I don't think people knew about who were ready to step up. A lot of those younger kids would have been starters on most other teams, but they may not have had the opportunity the year before because our 1992 team was so stacked."

Just three plays into the game, however, it looked like Troy was well on its way to producing the blowout many had expected.

On the third play from scrimmage, Troy junior Winfred Stafford broke free on a play behind left tackle Lewe Sessions—who would go on to play at Penn State University—and scampered fifty-three yards for a touchdown. Eric Stein—a converted soccer player—booted the extra point for the Trojans. And just like that, before many of the nine thousand fans in attendance that night had even settled into their seats, Troy already had jumped out to a 7–0 lead and appeared to be rolling to redemption.

Not quite.

Following Troy's early touchdown, Piqua's defense stiffened. Its defensive line—bolstered by sophomore Joey Lyman, who would go on to play at Miami University, and junior Antwon Jones, who would go on to play at Notre Dame—stymied Troy's offense the rest of the first half. Neither had played a key role for the Indians the year before, but they stepped up and were ready to shine when given the opportunity that season.

After Stafford's electrifying touchdown run, Troy gained just fourteen on the next eleven carries of the first half, and Stafford had just thirteen yards on his final six carries of the night. No Troy drive lasted more than 2:25 the rest of the half, and Piqua held a 14:54 to 9:06 edge in time of possession in the first half.

"Give them a lot of credit—they had a great game plan," Nolan said. "They did some things we hadn't seen before. I don't just mean we hadn't seen before that season—they did a few things we had never seen from Bill since he arrived there in 1995."

Troy's defense, meanwhile, kept the Trojans in the game. No matter, however, as Piqua answered Troy's touchdown with a special teams score. Bryan Magoteaux scored on a fifty-four-yard punt return late in the first quarter. The extra point was blocked, however, allowing Troy to maintain a 7–6 edge.

The punt return was not without controversy. To this day, many on Troy's side claim Magoteaux had signaled for a fair catch, meaning he shouldn't have been allowed to return the punt. Little did anyone know at the time, however, that was merely the first—and far less significant—referee's decision in the game.

Even with the two defenses controlling the game, Piqua was able to move the ball just enough to put Lyman in position to kick a thirty-one-yard field goal, giving the Indians a 9–7 lead going into halftime. And the game would stay that way until the fourth quarter.

In the fourth quarter, Troy's offense—thanks in part to a huge fourth-down gamble—finally was able to get rolling behind fullback Brad Clay. Troy marched the ball sixty-five yards in eleven plays early in the quarter. On fourth-and-eleven of that drive, Troy quarterback Gene Steinke found halfback Scot Brewer down the left sideline on a twenty-six-yard touchdown pass. Clay punched in the 2-point conversion to give the Trojans a 15–9 lead with 9:13 left to play in the game.

Piqua would get the ball back, but with 7:59 to play in the game, Johns—who had been largely perfect up to that point—threw his first interception of the night, which was picked off by Trojan defensive back Scott Young.

Troy marched into Piqua territory, converting a fourth-and-two near midfield to keep the drive alive. On third down, Steinke attempted another pass to Brewer. It appeared Brewer was run over by Piqua defender Ryan Honeycutt on the play, but no pass interference call was made. It was the second controversial play of the night—but again, not the one that ultimately would decide the game.

After Troy's punt, Piqua got the ball back on its own sixteen with just two minutes and forty-eight seconds to play. That's when Johns—who would go on to play at the University of Dayton before beginning a college coaching career that has since landed him the job as offensive coordinator at Indiana University—completely took over the game to forever write himself into the rivalry history books.

"When I threw that interception [to Young], I felt like the littlest guy in the room," Johns said in an interview with the *Troy Daily News* after the game. "I was begging the guys. We had to get the ball back. All I wanted was one last chance."

A twenty-one-yard scramble by Johns—who appeared to be trapped for a certain quarterback sack that would have all but ended the game—put the ball near midfield. On the next play, Troy was called for pass interference on a play Troy's side would argue wasn't nearly as egregious as the non-call on Brewer during the prior series. This gave the Indians the ball at the Trojan twenty-seven with just twenty-six seconds to play. It was the third—but not the last—controversial call of the night to go against the Trojans (in the eyes of Troy supporters, at least).

On the very next play, Johns tossed a beautiful twenty-two-yard pass to Magoteaux, giving the Indians the ball at the Trojan five-yard line with just seconds left in the game.

"It was a good pass," Magoteaux said in an interview after the game. "I split the seam and Kevin put it right between the defenders."

Honeycutt was given the ball on the next play, pushing the ball forward behind a surging Piqua line to the Trojan one, but appeared to stop short of the goal line as time expired. Troy was called for a facemasking penalty on the play, however, giving the Indians a final, untimed down.

It also gave steaming Troy fans one final piece of evidence that, in their mind, they had been cheated that night.

"All I thought was, 'Thank God' when I got the call," Honeycutt said.

On the final play of the game, Honeycutt bulled his way in for the score behind lineman Adam Baker. Lyman kicked the extra point with no time on the clock for the stunning—and, in the eyes of some, controversial—victory.

Troy fans remained up in arms for weeks after the game, flooding the local newspaper with Letters to the Editor about the way the game was officiated.

Nolan remained above the fray, however. "There were some calls that could have gone either way, but ultimately, we never should have allowed ourselves to get in that position," he said. "That was probably one of the most talented teams we've ever had here, but all most people remember is that we lost to Piqua and how we lost to Piqua. We had the opportunity to put the game away and never let it come down to a final play, but we didn't take advantage of those opportunities."

THE BATTLE ON THE MIAMI

Troy would blow out its final five opponents that season, but because of a one-point loss to its rival on the final play of the game, Troy finished the season 9-1, lost out on a chance at a GMVC title and missed qualifying for the playoffs.

Piqua also would finish the rest of the season undefeated, claiming the GMVC title the Trojans so desperately wanted.

Piqua—which had been moved down from Division I to Division II that season—also would make a lengthy playoff run, which came as a surprise to many, considering how much talent the Indians had lost from the year before. Piqua would easily defeat Lemon Monroe (32–16) and Franklin (35–14) in the first two playoff games, qualifying for the state semifinals for the third time in four years.

The loss would have a profound effect on Troy players—one that still lingers, in some form or another, for many of those players.

"It's something I still think about almost every day," Brewer said in 2007, by which time he had become a coach at his alma mater and Troy's defensive coordinator. "Usually when I'm standing there in the shower, it hits me."

The loss also would completely change Nolan's philosophy regarding the rivalry. "Honestly, when I got here, I really think we tried to treat the Troy-Piqua game like it was just another game," he said. "We didn't want to get the kids too hyped up and too nervous for the Troy-Piqua game. I think that 1993 game changed all of that for us. I think that's when we finally realized how big of a deal this was to both communities and there really was no such thing as hyping it up too much. We went 9-1 that year, but since we lost to Piqua, it felt like a bad season. On the other hand, if we had gone 1-9 and beat Piqua, I think people would have considered it a successful season because we beat Piqua. That's how big that game is around here."

That fundamental change in philosophy—along with a serious infusion of talent—would serve Nolan and the Trojans well in the coming years. Up to that point, the Indians had dominated the 1990s, winning three out of four rivalry matchups, including the coveted playoff victory in 1992. Better days were ahead for the Trojans—but not quite yet.

1994: Piqua 13, Troy 6

In 1994, the roles were reversed, as Piqua (which returned most of its starters from the year before) was the favorite and Troy (which lost most of its key components to graduation) was the prohibitive underdog. Troy nearly turned the tables on the Indians that season, falling just short in its upset bid.

In a game played at Troy Memorial Stadium, Piqua took a 10–0 halftime lead on a twelve-yard touchdown run by Magoteaux and a twenty-six-yard field goal by Lyman. Troy's defense—loaded with sophomores—held the Indians in check for the most part.

In the fourth quarter, Troy was finally able to get something against the Piqua defense, which had been dominant up to that point. The Trojans put together a nineteen-play, seventy-two-yard drive that was capped off by a three-yard touchdown run by Stafford. Piqua stuffed Troy's 2-point conversion attempt, leaving the Indians with a 10–6 lead.

Unfortunately for Troy, the drive ate 8:02 off the clock, leaving just 3:44 to play in the game. Troy attempted an onside kick, which Piqua's Sheldon Steinke pounced on. Soon after, Honeycutt broke loose on a thirty-six-yard run that set up a thirty-one-yard field goal by Lyman, extending Piqua's lead to 13–6.

With time running out, Troy quarterback Jason Massingill hooked up with receivers A.J. McMullen, Jason Houck and Justin Smith for gains of seven, twelve and thirteen yards, respectively, putting the ball at the Indian twenty-six with just thirty-two seconds to play.

On the very next play, Magoteaux intercepted a pass near the goal line, sealing the victory for Piqua. It would be Piqua's fifth win in six tries against the Trojans, as well as its third in a row.

Troy would finish the season 6-4. Piqua would close out the regular season 10-0, win the GMVC title and open the Division II playoffs with wins over Cincinnati Anderson (31–3) and Celina (14–7), putting the Indians in the state semifinals for the fourth time in five years. Buckeye Local defeated Piqua 21–14 in the state semifinals.

Things were about to change for the Trojans, however—and history was about to be made the following year.

1995: Troy 17, Piqua 14 (overtime)

With so many young players up and down the roster, the Trojans entered the 1995 season largely a question mark. Little did anyone know that over the next four years, that question mark would become an exclamation point as the Trojans racked up four league titles, four wins over Piqua and three trips

THE BATTLE ON THE MIAMI

to the postseason and produced two legends and some of the most decorated talents in school history.

No one could possibly have known how things were going to turn out heading into that season, however. The Trojans featured two underclassmen in the backfield: freshman halfback Ryan Brewer—the younger brother of Scot and the first freshman ever to start on varsity for Nolan—and sophomore fullback Matt Dallman. All they would do is go on to become two of the top three rushers in school history.

The defense was anchored by junior Jason Manson, who had played as a sophomore but remained largely an unknown quantity. All he would do would be become a two-time Southwest District Defensive Player of the Year and the Associated Press Division I Co-Defensive Player of the Year in 1996.

But again, no one could have possibly known any of that at the time.

As expected, the young Trojans faced their fair share of challenges early. Troy would need overtime to win its first two games of the season, defeating Springfield North 22–12 in overtime in the season opener and Cincinnati Anderson 33–22 in overtime the following week.

Certainly Troy wouldn't play any more overtime games that season, right? Wrong.

Perhaps battle-tested by those first two games, Troy rolled through its next three games, blowing out Toledo Rogers, West Carrollton and Vandalia, setting up the annual rivalry game with Piqua in front of nine thousand fans at Wertz Field. Not only would those nine thousand fans get four quarters' worth of back-and-forth action, but they'd also get a little extra to boot.

Troy dominated the entire first half on both sides of the ball. Dallman and Brewer showed signs of what was to come in the following years as Dallman racked up 96 of his game-high 113 yards in the first half, while Brewer added touchdown runs of 13 and 20 yards. Nick Trostle kicked both extra points after Brewer's touchdowns, giving the Trojans what appeared to be a comfortable 14–0 lead.

"The first half, they seemed confused by our motion," Dallman said in an interview with the *Troy Daily News* after the game. "They weren't filling the gaps, but in the second half they started using more stunts and filling the holes faster."

Piqua's defense would indeed hold the Trojans scoreless in the second half, but the Trojans' defense—led by Manson, who finished the night with an astounding seven tackles for loss—played lights out as well until late in the fourth quarter.

That's when Piqua's offense finally started clicking behind quarterback Rob Lillicrap. He led the Indians on a seventy-four-yard drive that culminated in a thirteen-yard touchdown pass to Sheldon Steinke with five minutes and thirty-seven seconds to play, cutting Troy's lead in half, 14–7.

Minutes later, Piqua linebacker Lance Karn picked off a Troy pass and returned it to the Trojan twenty, setting up a four-yard touchdown pass from Lillicrap to Kevin Darner with 3:51 to play. Lyman's extra point tied the game at 14–14.

The game would stay that way through the end of regulation, forcing the first overtime game in rivalry history. With both teams receiving alternate possessions, Troy got the ball first in overtime but couldn't score a touchdown. Instead, the Trojans were forced to settle for a twenty-five-yard field goal by Nick Trostle, following a clutch eleven-yard pass from Massingill to Joe Williamson to put the Trojans in field position.

"Sure, I was nervous. I'm nervous with all of them," Trostle said in an interview after the game. He had kicked the game-winning PAT in the overtime win over Springfield South and the game-winning field goal in the overtime win over Cincinnati Anderson. "Every kick is a big one, but this kick meant everything because it was the Piqua game. I've been going to this game for as long as I can remember, but I was always in the stands. I could never see myself in this situation."

With the Trojans up 17–14, Piqua got the ball at the twenty-yard line, needing either a touchdown for the victory or a field goal to send the game into a second overtime. Troy's defense would stuff the Indians three yards short of a first down, forcing the Indians to attempt the field goal. Lyman who had kicked crucial field goals in each of Piqua's wins the previous two years—missed from thirty yards, sealing the win for the Trojans.

"I knew Trostle would hit it," Dallman said. "I knew it as soon as he walked out on the field."

Piqua would finish the season 8-2. Troy would finish the regular season 9-1, capturing a share of the GMVC title. In the opening round of the playoffs, Toledo St. Francis would defeat Troy, 16–6.

1996: Troy 48, Piqua 0

Going into the 1996 season, expectations were high for the Trojans, who were state-ranked in preseason polls and celebrating the 100th anniversary

THE BATTLE ON THE MIAMI

of Troy football. The Trojans returned nearly every starter from the previous season and would receive an added talent boost from sophomore tight end/linebacker Kris Dielman, who had played on the freshman team the season before.

Dielman, as it would turn out, was a star in the making. He would start at tight end three years for the Trojans. In Troy's run-heavy offense, he wouldn't receive many receiving opportunities, but he became a fixture as a powerful, relentless blocker for the Trojans.

"He's probably the best blocker I ever coached," Nolan would say years later. "He was just absolutely dominant. He was basically like having a third tackle out there. He would take over games from his tight end position. Opposing teams had to come up with game plans just to figure out a way to deal with him."

With all that talent in place, Troy was never seriously tested in the regular season—including in its rivalry game against Piqua. Troy simply rolled over the Indians, 48–0, producing the decade's only blowout victory.

Manson set the tone early for the Trojans, blocking a punt deep in Piqua territory. Troy's Travis Lucas fell on the blocked punt, setting up the Trojans' second touchdown of the game. Defensively, Piqua had no answer for the one-two punch of Dallman and Brewer, who had since matured into one of the top backfields in the state. Up 21–0 early, Troy quarterback Shawn Gregory connected with Brian Dunn on a Hail Mary touchdown pass just before halftime to seal Piqua's fate.

The Indians would finish the regular season 7-3. Troy would finish the regular season 10-0. At the end of the regular season, Troy was the no. 1–ranked Division I team in Ohio and the no. 8 team in *USA Today*'s national rankings. In the postseason, however, Troy's dream season would come to an end with a 13–10 loss to eventual state champion Lima Senior in the Division I regional championship game.

1997: Troy 28, Piqua 10

The following season, Troy lost many of its key components on defense but returned Brewer and Dallman in the backfield, along with a massive offensive line led by future Ohio University tackle Chris Jackson.

Troy simply outscored the opposition all season, averaging more than fifty points per game. That season, Brewer would set a school single-season rushing record with 2,336 yards, breaking the record set by Troy legend Bob Ferguson. Dallman wasn't far behind with 1,724 yards, as he joined Ferguson as one of only two running backs to rush for more than 1,000 yards in three consecutive seasons. Brewer would join that club a year later.

Troy's dynamic backfield duo would again prove to be too much for the Indians in 1997, as the two scored all of Troy's touchdowns in a 28–10 victory. Piqua would finish the season 8-2, while Troy would again finish 10-0 before falling to Worthington Kilbourne in the opening round of the playoffs.

1998: Troy 31, Piqua 14

The 1998 season would be Brewer and Dielman's swan song. Brewer would rush for a then–state record 2,856 yards, winning the coveted Mr. Football Ohio award. Dielman, in addition to playing tight end, would also play linebacker full time for the first time in his career, earning All-Ohio honors.

Piqua, meanwhile, remained on the rebound but showed glimpses of its stars of the future in halfback Scott Foster and defensive back/running back Scott Rohrbach.

Brewer and Dielman were as good as advertised in the 1998 game, with Brewer rushing for more than two hundred yards and Dielman taking over the game on both sides of the ball, feasting on Piqua's defensive line as a blocking tight end and recording double-digit tackles at linebacker.

As good as they were, however, it was a relatively unheralded Trojan player who sealed the game. In the fourth quarter, Troy led 24–14, but Piqua was driving for a touchdown that would have cut into the Trojans' lead. Trojan cornerback Pete Johnston—a converted quarterback—stepped in front of Piqua quarterback Richie Pearson's pass in the end zone, returning it 107 yards for a touchdown to seal the game.

Piqua would finish the regular season 7-3, while Troy would finish 8-2 and capture a fourth straight conference title, an unprecedented feat in school history. Brewer—after several recruiting fiascos that saw him overlooked by nearly every Division I program in the country—would end up at the University of South Carolina. Dielman would go on to play at Indiana University as both a tight end and defensive tackle. Following his playing days at Indiana, Dielman would sign with the San Diego Chargers as an undrafted free agent. He would move to offensive guard, a position he had never played before, where he would become a five-time Pro Bowl selection.

THE BATTLE ON THE MIAMI

1999: Piqua 30, Troy 25

The Golden Age of the rivalry closed in 1999 with a game at Wertz Stadium. By that time, much of Troy's incredible run of talent had passed through the pipeline. Piqua, meanwhile was just getting started on another major run.

That year, Rohrbach put on a virtuoso performance against the Trojans, returning a kickoff eighty yards to set up one Piqua touchdown and scoring another on a long touchdown reception. Troy stayed close throughout much of the night against the heavily favored Indians, but a late fumble allowed Piqua to wrap up the 30–25 victory.

Troy would finish the season 4-6—its first losing season under Nolan—while Piqua would finish the regular season 10-0 before losing to Anthony Wayne in the first round of the playoffs.

And so wrapped up what many consider the greatest decade in the history of the rivalry.

"It was a pretty incredible run by both teams," Nees said. "You could make an argument for other decades being as good, but I think it would be a pretty tough argument, considering the amount of talent that went through both programs and what both teams were able to accomplish during the 1990s."

The rivalry wasn't exactly dead, however. There would still be a few more classics left—including a battle to kick off the millennium that saw a final meeting between two playoff teams.

Chapter 9
TO THE PRESENT

2000–2014

It was the dawn of a new millennium in Miami County, but one thing remained constant in 2000: Troy and Piqua both still were churning out quality football teams.

Action from the 2011 Troy-Piqua game. *Courtesy of Lee Woolery/Speedshot Photo.*

THE BATTLE ON THE MIAMI

Piqua running back Trent Yeomans looks for room to run in 2013. *Courtesy of Lee Woolery/Speedshot Photo.*

The rivalry's "golden decade" was one year in the past, but both teams would churn out top-notch football teams in 2000 before hitting a downslide. The best was to come for Piqua—the Indians would win a Division II state championship in 2006—but 2000 would be the first year both could claim a playoff team and a league contender in the same year.

Troy would hit a serious downturn the next three years, going 4-6 in 2001 and 3-7 in both 2002 and 2003 before rebounding to make the playoffs in

2004. Piqua would hit its own rough patch before its run to a state title as well, going 4-6 in 2002 and 2004, the Indians' first-ever losing seasons under Bill Nees and their first losing season overall since 1985.

But before that, they would meet a final time in 2000, the final meeting to date with both teams at the height of their powers.

2000: Troy 24, Piqua 14

It was a cold January night in 2001 when the Troy and Piqua basketball teams met inside Piqua's Garby Gymnasium. Despite the action taking place in front of them on the hardwood, however, very few of the fans sitting in the Troy student section seemed particularly interested in talking about basketball.

Midway through the second quarter, the Trojan students began chanting at the Piqua student section sitting in the stands across the floor: "First in state, second in county! First in state, second in county!"

The message was clear, if not particularly accurate.

The previous fall, the Piqua football team had made an incredible run to the Division II state championship game—the first such trip to the state finals in school history—only to lose to Olmstead Falls in the title game, 21-0. During the course of that run, however, Piqua had lost to Troy—which qualified for the Division I playoffs that year—in the regular season.

So even on a night when basketball should have been taking center stage—which, in a literal sense, it was—Troy fans wanted to point out that no matter what Piqua had accomplished during the postseason (even if the Trojan faithful didn't quite get their facts straight), it didn't erase the loss to Troy.

Such is part of the beauty of the Troy-Piqua rivalry—the winning team gets bragging rights for an entire year, regardless of what else may transpire after the game.

When the two teams met in 2000, it had all the trappings of a typical big game within the rivalry. The two teams came in with identical 6-1 records, and both were in the hunt for a conference title. Both teams had plenty of star power, as well. Troy had the dynamic duo of halfback William Block and fullback Dave Levorchick—both of whom would rush for more than one thousand yards that season—in the backfield and two-way lineman Kris Mick. Piqua was led by halfback Scott Foster—who would become the first player in school history to rush for more than two thousand yards that season—on offense and blue chip recruit Quinn Pitcock on the defensive line.

Despite all that star power, however, the game was won in the trenches. Troy's offensive line—which included junior Mick and senior Tim Summers at one tackle, senior Josh Smith at the other tackle, senior Josh Mays and junior Adam Ritter and guards and senior Ben Beitzel at center—controlled Pitcock and the rest of the Piqua defensive line from beginning to end.

"They showed tremendous heart in that game," Nolan said. "We were able to line up and win the battle at the line of scrimmage. Any time you can do that, you are going to win some football games. It was an incredible effort by those kids against a great Piqua defensive line."

Troy jumped out to an early lead when junior halfback Josh Carnes—who frequently got lost in the shuffle in the backfield with Block and Levorchick, despite rushing for more than seven hundred yards that season—ripped off a forty-eight-yard touchdown run on the game's opening drive. Joe Wolke knocked through the extra point to put the Trojans up 7–0.

The Trojans would extend that lead to 14–0 in the fourth quarter by putting together an eight-play, seventy-one-yard drive. Block did much of the heavy lifting with a twenty-one-yard run to set up a one-yard touchdown run by Levorchick.

Troy's defense, meanwhile, was able to keep Piqua's offense under wraps for most of the first half. Going into the game on the heels of a 42–17 blowout loss to Butler the week before, Nolan made a personnel change that paid immediate dividends against Piqua. That week, Block and Levorchick both began splitting time between offense and defense, with Block playing the entire game on defense at cornerback and Levorchick going the entire way at middle linebacker.

Following Troy's second touchdown drive, however, Piqua finally was able to get something going on offense. Foster ripped off runs of fifteen and sixteen yards following the kickoff, while quarterback John Pearson hooked up with receiver Austin Netzley for a fourteen-yard gain. That moved the Indians into Trojan territory, where Pearson hooked up with Pitcock—who had been inserted into the game at tight end—on a nine-yard touchdown pass. Brad Erwin's extra point cut Troy's lead in half, 14–7.

Late in the third quarter, Troy took over at its own forty-two. From there, Troy hammered away at the Piqua defense with Block, Levorchick and Carnes, putting together a fifteen-play drive that culminated in a two-yard touchdown run by Carnes, his second of the night. Wolke's extra point made it 21–7 with ten minutes and twenty-eight seconds left to play in the game.

OHIO'S TROY VS. PIQUA FOOTBALL RIVALRY

A late defensive stand by Troy would ensure Piqua would never threaten again. The Indians drove down to the Trojan twenty-eight-yard line, where Pearson dumped off a pass to Foster. Foster was stopped just inches short of the first down marker, however, giving the Trojans the ball back. A fifty-five-yard run by block set up a twenty-six-yard field goal by Wolke to ice the game.

Troy would close out the regular season with wins over Northmont and Greenville to earn a share of the GMVC title and a spot in the Division I regional quarterfinals. Troy would defeat Miamisburg 47–14 in its playoff opener and then fall to eventual state champion Upper Arlington the next week, 42–14.

Like Troy, Piqua would win its final two regular season games, also clinching a share of the conference crown and earning a spot in the Division II playoffs. The Indians got on a roll in the postseason, beating Oxford Talawanda (54–33), Loveland (28–17) and Butler (17–15) to earn a Division II regional title and a spot in the state semifinals for the fifth time in school history. Unlike their previous four trips, however, the Indians were successful in their fifth trip to the state semifinals, knocking off Marysville 18–7 to earn the school's first-ever trip to the state championship game. Piqua would lose to Olmstead Falls in the state title game—a fact that would seemingly be lost on Troy's student section at the subsequent basketball game between the two schools a little more than a month later.

AND THAT WOULD BE IT, in terms of both Troy and Piqua meeting atop the mountain. Troy would have several nice runs of its own later in the century, earning playoff berths in 2004, 2010 and 2011. Piqua, in addition to its state title in 2006, would reach the postseason in 2007 as well. But never again would the two teams face each other during banner seasons with a league title and playoff berths on the line.

All they were left playing for during the rest of the century was pride and bragging rights. But when it comes to the Troy-Piqua rivalry, that is usually more than enough.

When the two teams met in 2001, Piqua was in the midst of another playoff run, while Troy was mired in its second 4-6 season in three years. This time, there would be no heroic performance by the underdogs. There would be no last-play touchdown to win the game and no interception to end the game. It was a blowout.

With Pitcock leading the way, Piqua's defense turned in an inspired effort. The Indians allowed just one first down the entire first half and had given up just three for the entire game until late in the contest when Troy was able to get the ball moving long after Piqua's starters already had retired to the bench.

Troy ran twenty-seven plays in the first half for a grand total of fifteen yards in total offense—thirteen of which came on a run by Carnes for Troy's only first down. Troy didn't cross its own thirty-four in the first half and didn't cross midfield until the final series of the game. All that added up to a 28–0 win for the Indians—their first shutout of Troy since 1975.

Troy would finish the season 4-6, while Piqua would go 9-1, earning another trip to the playoffs. The Indians defeated Edgewood 21–0 in the regional quarterfinals before falling to Vandalia-Butler, 30–0, in the regional semifinals.

The following year, in 2002, Piqua would finish the regular season 4-6, while the Trojans would go 3-7. A testament to the rich history and continued success of both programs, it was the first time both teams had finished with a losing record in the same year since 1979—a span of twenty-three years.

With little else to play for, the two teams slugged it out in a game that wasn't decided until the fourth quarter. Piqua got on the board early on a twenty-three-yard field goal by Joey Hudson. The score would remain 3–0 going into halftime.

Piqua took the opening kickoff of the second half and marched down the field, with quarterback Ryan Karn carrying the ball in from twelve yards out on a quarterback bootleg, putting the Indians up 9–0. Troy would answer on the ensuing kickoff, when Rob Byrer's seventy-four-yard return set up a one-yard touchdown run by Adam Bornhorst, cutting Piqua's lead to 9–6.

Troy would drive deep into Piqua territory three more times on the night, but one ended when Karn recovered a fumble and two more ended after failed conversion attempts on fourth down.

The 2003 contest between the Trojans and Indians would be remembered as much for what happened in the skies above as for what happened on the field below. Just after the opening kickoff at Troy Memorial Stadium, lightning filled the skies, and the game was postponed until the following night—making it the first two-day affair in the history of the rivalry.

Once play resumed Saturday night, Piqua took the lead early on a Hudson field goal. Troy would answer later in the half, tying the game on a Matt Noll field goal.

Late in the third quarter, a pair of long runs by Karn set up the game's only touchdown, a two-yard run by Brian Snyder, giving the Indians a 10–3 lead.

OHIO'S TROY VS. PIQUA FOOTBALL RIVALRY

The score would stay that way until the game's final moments. Troy put together a drive deep into Piqua territory. On fourth down, Troy quarterback Jared Blackmore attempted a pass to receiver Shane Carter in the back of the end zone. Carter caught the ball, but Hudson broke it up in midair, preserving the Indians' 10–3 victory.

The following year, Troy would snap a three-game losing streak to the Indians, thanks in large part to the running of halfback Cody Boyd and a key turnover set up by a pair of future college linemen.

On the second play of the game, Piqua's Kyle Blair scored on a thirty-five-yard touchdown run. Troy would answer with a field goal by Mark Cermak, cutting Piqua's lead to 7–3. Piqua appeared to be driving for another score when Troy defensive lineman Ryan Custer (who would go on to play at Vanderbilt) shot the gap and forced a fumble, which fellow defensive lineman Todd Denlinger (who would play at Ohio State) pounced on at the Trojan thirty-one.

That sparked a Trojan drive that would end in a twenty-two-yard touchdown pass from Troy quarterback A.J. Bush to fullback Dustin Messer, putting the Trojans up 10–7 going into halftime.

In the second half, it was all Troy. With Piqua focused on stopping Boyd—who would finish with more than 150 rushing yards and a 36-yard touchdown run—Bush completed a touchdown pass to T.J. White. Following Boyd's touchdown, Messer broke loose on a 66-yard touchdown scamper to ice the game.

Piqua would finish the season 4-6 with a sophomore-laden team, while Troy would make its return to the playoffs for the first time since 2000, falling to Westerville South in the regional quarterfinals.

In 2005, the two teams would meet in another classic that wasn't decided until Piqua's Jafe Pitcock—the younger brother of All-American Quinn Pitcock—blocked a Troy field goal late in the fourth quarter, allowing the Indians to hold on for a 13–12 victory.

"I had gotten through every other time and I just knew I had to get in there and get it down," Pitcock said after the game. "Pete [Rolf] had his guy out and I had a straight shot. I just dove got my hands out and blocked it. It was great. It's the best feeling ever. No words can describe the Piqua-Troy game, no words."

The 2006 Piqua team featured what many consider the greatest assemblage of talent ever to play at Piqua. Tailback Brandon Saine—who would rush for a school-record 2,287 yards that season—would earn Mr. Football Ohio honors that year. Saine, however, was far from the only

The action is always hard-hitting when Troy and Piqua play, as seen in this 2013 photo. *Courtesy of Lee Woolery/Speedshot Photo.*

weapon on that team, as more than a dozen players would go on to play at the college level, including nearly a half dozen who would become Division I college football players.

At quarterback that year was junior Justin Hemm, who would graduate from Piqua with every school passing record. His favorite target was senior

Phil Collier, who would set a school single-season receiving yardage record that season. All-conference tackle Ben Davis anchored the offensive line.

Defensively, Piqua had three defensive linemen—Jafe Pitcock, Dominic Allen and Dusty Snyder—win all-conference awards that season. The Rolf brothers, Pete and David, anchored the outside linebacker position. Both would go on to become Division I college football players.

"It was a pretty special team that we had that year," Nees said. "Not only was it a talented team, but it was a close-knit team as well. It was probably one of the closest teams I've ever been around. And I think that translated well on the field."

It certainly did against Troy. Not that the Indians needed any extra motivation for the game, but they got it the night before the game when a group of teenage Troy fans snuck into Piqua's Alexander Stadium and spray-painted derogatory remarks about the Indians on the playing field. That was all it took.

Piqua scored on a 69-yard pass from Hemm to Collier on its first offense play, and from that point, it was off to the races as Piqua cruised to a 42–7

Troy and Piqua players battle for a loose ball in 2012. *Courtesy of Lee Woolery/Speedshot Photo.*

THE BATTLE ON THE MIAMI

Troy and Piqua battle at the line of scrimmage in 2012. *Courtesy of Lee Woolery/Speedshot Photo.*

victory. Collier finished the game with three catches for 113 yards and two scores. Saine had 110 rushing yards and 73 receiving yards. Hemm completed seven of eleven passes for 198 yards and four touchdowns.

Following the Troy game, Piqua would finish the regular season 8-2, good enough for a spot in the Division II playoffs. As good as Piqua was during the regular season, the Indians truly caught fire in the postseason.

In its first playoff game, Piqua blew out Toledo Central Catholic, 33–14. In the next game, Piqua beat Wapakoneta 40–21. In the regional title game, the Indians blanked Ashland 27–0. In the state semifinals, Piqua blew past Turpin 22–9. And finally, in the Division II state championship game, Piqua defeated Pickerington Central 26–7 to become the state champions of Ohio.

In terms of the Troy-Piqua rivalry, however, that would be the Indians' highlight for the next five years.

The following season, Piqua came into the rivalry game 7-1, well on its way to a second consecutive playoff berth. Troy, meanwhile, stumbled in at

OHIO'S TROY VS. PIQUA FOOTBALL RIVALRY

Troy sacks Piqua's quarterback in 2010. *Courtesy of Lee Woolery/Speedshot Photo.*

3-5, heaving lost its last three in a row. Once again, it appeared a blowout was about to happen.

When Piqua jumped out to a quick 14–0 lead, it appeared those suspicions would be confirmed. What followed, however, was one of the greatest comebacks—and one of the greatest finishes—in rivalry history.

With Troy's offensive line—tackles Jake Current and T.J. White, center Alex Baker and guards Joe Brading and Daniel Shaw—leading the way, senior tailback Corey Brown had a career night, carrying the ball more than forty times for more than three hundred yards and four touchdowns. His second to last touchdown of the night put the Trojans up 28–27 midway through the fourth quarter. Piqua's Ryan Musselman would return the ensuing kickoff eighty-two yards for a touchdown, however, and Hemm would run in the 2-point conversion, giving Piqua a 35–28 lead and setting up a final miracle drive for the Trojans.

THE BATTLE ON THE MIAMI

Right: Troy celebrates a fumble recovery in 2009. *Courtesy of Lee Woolery/Speedshot Photo.*

Below: The blood drive between the two cities is an annual part of the Troy-Piqua rivalry, in 2011. *Courtesy of Lee Woolery/Speedshot Photo.*

Above: A Trojan defender tackles a Piqua ball carrier during the 2013 game. *Courtesy of Lee Woolery/Speedshot Photo.*

Left: Troy's Joe Brading celebrates after a win over Piqua in 2008. *Courtesy of Lee Woolery/Speedshot Photo.*

THE BATTLE ON THE MIAMI

Troy coach Steve Nolan talks with Troy quarterback Tyler Wright during the Troy-Piqua game in 2008. *Courtesy of Lee Woolery/Speedshot Photo.*

Brown was tremendous on the drive, carrying the load and scoring the game's final touchdown. Rather than go for the tie and play overtime, Nolan elected to go for two, with quarterback Tyler Wright completing a pass to Benson McGillvary, giving the Trojans the win.

"That night was probably one of the greatest nights of my life," Baker said after the game. "I'll never forget that as long as I live."

That game would kick-start a five-game winning streak for the Trojans—and allow Nolan to close out his career at Troy in style. Matt Allen would nearly

OHIO'S TROY VS. PIQUA FOOTBALL RIVALRY

duplicate Brown's effort the next year, rushing for 287 yards and four touchdowns in Troy's 49–28 win over the Indians.

In 2009, Marcus Foster recorded a pair of touchdowns, Kyle Terando returned a punt for a touchdown and Troy's defense shut out Piqua for the first time since 1996 as the Trojans cruised to a 26–0 victory.

The following year, Troy picked up its fourth win in a row over the Indians, 27–14. Troy quarterback Cody May connected with his favorite target, Ian Dunaway, on a touchdown pass; Brad Armstrong returned an interception forty-six yards for a touchdown; Ashlin Stoltz kicked a pair of field goals; and fullback Zach Jones scored on a late touchdown run to ice the game for the Trojans.

In 2011, Troy scored its fifth victory in a row over the Indians. Isaiah Williams rushed for two touchdowns, Foster added one and May again hooked up with Dunaway for

Top: Troy fans celebrate a Trojan score in 2014. *Courtesy of Lee Woolery/Speedshot Photo.*

Left: A Piqua ball carrier battles for extra yards in 2012. *Courtesy of Lee Woolery/Speedshot Photo.*

THE BATTLE ON THE MIAMI

Right: Troy running back Matt Allen breaks through the Piqua line for a touchdown in 2008. *Courtesy of Lee Woolery/ Speedshot Photo.*

Below: Troy and Piqua captains prior to the coin toss in 2008. *Courtesy of Lee Woolery/ Speedshot Photo.*

OHIO'S TROY VS. PIQUA FOOTBALL RIVALRY

Left: The Troy-Piqua game is part of the Great American Rivalry Series, sponsored by the U.S. Marines. *Courtesy of Lee Woolery/Speedshot Photo.*

Below, left: Troy quarterback Cody May (left) and receiver Ian Dunaway celebrate after a touchdown pass against Piqua in 2011. *Courtesy of Lee Woolery/Speedshot Photo.*

Below, right: Piqua quarterback Cole Selsor looks for an open receiver in 2010. *Courtesy of Lee Woolery/Speedshot Photo.*

THE BATTLE ON THE MIAMI

Above: Troy's defense wraps up a Piqua ball carrier in 2011. *Courtesy of Lee Woolery/ Speedshot Photo.*

Right: Troy quarterback Cody May looks to deliver a pass against Piqua in 2011. *Courtesy of Lee Woolery/ Speedshot Photo.*

Above: Troy's captains are greeted by members of the U.S. Marines prior to the coin toss in 2011. *Courtesy of Lee Woolery/Speedshot Photo*

Left: Troy running back Nick James carries the ball against Piqua in 2011. *Courtesy of Lee Woolery/Speedshot Photo.*

a touchdown as Troy beat Piqua 27–7. Much as it had in 2010, Troy would again go to the playoffs in 2011, losing in the first round.

One month after the season ended, so did an era. In December 2011, Nolan announced his retirement after twenty-eight years of coaching at Troy High School. He retired holding nearly every coaching record in school history and a number of impressive stats. One number stands out among the rest, however: during his coaching career, Steve Nolan went 17-12 against his team's greatest rival.

Following Nolan's departure in 2011, former Troy running back Scot Brewer became head coach of the Trojans. Brewer served as coach through 2014. Matt Burgbacher was named Troy's new head coach in the winter of 2015. Since Nolan's retirement, the Indians have gone on a

Troy and Piqua battle along the line of scrimmage in 2014. *Courtesy of Lee Woolery/ Speedshot Photo.*

OHIO'S TROY VS. PIQUA FOOTBALL RIVALRY

This page: Action from the 2011 Troy-Piqua game. *Courtesy of Lee Woolery/Speedshot Photo.*

THE BATTLE ON THE MIAMI

Troy's Jordan Delehanty (43) looks to get past a Piqua blocker in 2011. *Courtesy of Lee Woolery/ Speedshot Photo.*

Action from the 2012 Troy-Piqua game. *Courtesy of Lee Woolery/ Speedshot Photo.*

Troy's Brandon Lee waits on the ball against Piqua in 2014. *Courtesy of Lee Woolery/Speedshot Photo.*

Troy and Piqua battle along the line of scrimmage in 2014. *Courtesy of Lee Woolery/Speedshot Photo.*

Piqua's Trent Yeomans is congratulated by a member of the U.S. Marines after earning MVP honors for the Troy-Piqua game in 2013. *Courtesy of Lee Woolery/ Speedshot Photo.*

Piqua quarterback Dan Monnin delivers a pass in 2013. *Courtesy of Lee Woolery/ Speedshot Photo.*

Action from the 2013 Troy-Piqua game. *Courtesy of Lee Woolery/ Speedshot Photo.*

Action from the 2012 Troy-Piqua game. *Courtesy of Lee Woolery/ Speedshot Photo.*

THE BATTLE ON THE MIAMI

three-game winning streak of their own, beating Troy 14–0, 33–27 and, most recently, 41–10.

And so, after 130 meetings between the two teams, things are right back where they started before that first game in 1899: deadlocked. After more than a century of battles, the series between Ohio's most prolific rivals is tied, 62-62-6.

It seems only right.

Chapter 10
LEGENDS OF THE FALL

PIQUA'S GREATEST PLAYERS

CRAIG CLEMONS

It's somewhat ironic that one of the greatest players in Piqua High School football history would draw his early inspiration from three Troy High School legends.

"I remember when I was a boy, my best friend and I used to walk down County Road 25-A to get from Piqua to Troy," Craig Clemons said. "I remember at the edge of town near Troy, they had a sign honoring Troy's college All-Americans. They had a sign with the names Bob Ferguson, Tommy Myers and Tommy Vaughn on it. I remember thinking that one day I wanted to be able to do something to get my name on a sign outside of Piqua."

Craig Clemons would have been a star in any city, in any state, on any football team. As fate would have it, however, he was a star in Piqua, which turned out to be the perfect situation. In fact, the way Clemons sees it, growing up in Piqua and playing for the Indians was nothing short of divine intervention.

"Piqua was the perfect place for me to grow up," said Clemons, a 1968 Piqua High School graduate who went on to be a star football player at the University of Iowa and play for six years in the NFL, all with the Chicago Bears. "God put me in the perfect situation to grow up. It was safe; it was respectful. The Lord put me in Piqua, Ohio, for a reason. I had great teachers, great coaches and met great people in high school.

THE BATTLE ON THE MIAMI

"You have to remember, in those days there was a lot of unrest in this country. You had the Vietnam War, you had draft dodging, you had civil unrest. As a black man growing up, I felt like I didn't have to deal with a lot of that in Piqua. It was the perfect situation for me."

It was a situation Clemons took full advantage of in high school. A running back and hard-hitting defensive back blessed with size and speed, Clemons was a two-time team captain and an All-Ohio selection his senior year. He helped lead the Indians to a Miami Valley League title, was a two-time All-MVL selection and was picked to play in the Ohio All-State Football all-star game following his senior season. He also was a star on the basketball court—Clemons describes basketball as his "true love"—and was a charter member of the Piqua High School Athletic Hall of Fame in 1995.

"I go back to Piqua often," Clemons said. "I still have brothers, sisters and cousins who live in Piqua. I love going back and seeing them. I go back two or three times a year. I go back every Labor Day weekend; this event [the Piqua-Troy game] just happens to coincide with that."

Clemons cites former Piqua head coach Chuck Asher and freshman football coach Dick Pearson as two men who heavily influenced his young football career. "I learned everything I needed to know about the game of football while I was at Piqua," Clemons said. "I understood the game plan and was receptive to change. I learned a lot from Coach Asher and Coach Pearson. All in all, Piqua was the perfect situation for me as an athlete, too."

In fact, Clemons remembers that when Piqua played against its rival Troy, Asher would sometimes come up with unique ways to motivate his star player.

"When I was in high school, I wanted to play for USC," Clemons remembers. "They had a lot of great running backs at USC, and I wanted to be the next great running back for the Trojans. I remember one year before the Troy game, Coach Asher told me there were going to be scouts from USC in the crowd watching the game. It's kind of funny…I don't remember any scouts from USC being there, and nobody from USC ever contacted me."

Following his playing days at Piqua, Clemons went on to play at the University of Iowa, where he excelled as a defensive back. As a senior in 1971, Clemons was a first-team All-American, first-team All–Big Ten, team captain and was voted the team's most valuable player. While playing for the Hawkeyes, he also was second-team All–Big Ten as a sophomore and junior. Clemons was named to Iowa's All-Time Team.

He played in a pair of all-star games following graduation and was named MVP of both the Blue-Gray Classic and the Senior Bowl All-Star game. He also played in the Chicago Tribune All-Star contest, which featured a team of college all-stars taking on the NFL champions.

Clemons was taken by the Bears with the twelfth overall pick in the 1972 NFL draft—one pick ahead of NFL Hall of Fame running back Franco Harris. He would play six years with the Bears.

Clemons and his wife, Theresa, have three children—Stephanie, Jonathan and Jennifer—and six grandchildren.

Dr. Dave Gallagher

More than four decades ago, Dave Gallagher—a talented defensive lineman for the Piqua High School football team—had his choice of college powerhouses. In the end, he narrowed his list down to three: the University of Michigan, Duke University and Northwestern University.

Duke and Northwestern? Hardly among the college football elite.

But even as a high school student and one of the top football players in the state, Gallagher was looking for more than just a chance to play football. "My final three choices were Northwestern, Duke and Michigan," Gallagher said in an interview with the *Piqua Daily Call*. "Those were three of the top medical schools in the country and I had always wanted to be a doctor."

As talented as he was on the football field, Dr. Gallagher always put academics first. Eventually, he settled on a school that would allow him to excel both on the football field and in the classroom. Becoming a Wolverine paid off on both fronts for the 1970 Piqua High School graduate, who went on to become an All-American defensive tackle in college and was a first-round draft pick in the 1974 NFL draft. While playing in the NFL, he earned his medical degree from the University of Michigan.

"It came down to the fact that Duke and Northwestern were good schools academically and Michigan, obviously, was what it was—and what it still is," Dr. Gallagher said. "I knew I could have gone to Duke or Northwestern and played. But I knew that even if I went to Michigan and sat the bench, it was a great program. Plus, it's awfully hard to say no to Bo Schembechler."

Long before he became Dr. Gallagher, he may as well have been known as "Doctor Death" on the football field for the Indians. Gallagher was a force on both sides of the ball for the Indians, capturing All–Miami Valley League honors on both offense and defense. He won the school's Battered Helmet Award in 1969.

THE BATTLE ON THE MIAMI

"Obviously my football career started in large part thanks to [former Piqua coach] Chuck Asher," Dr. Gallagher said. "He had just come to the school when I was in the sixth grade, and he brought a new life and new spirit to the program. Right off the bat, he made the program into a winner. He was the kind of coach that you wanted to play for, that you wanted to please."

As good as Gallagher was on the football field, however, his scholarship offer from Michigan came after then–assistant coach Gary Moeller saw Gallagher play in a basketball game for the Indians. During his time at Piqua, Gallagher was captain of the football, basketball and track teams.

"Gary Moeller—who eventually went on to become the head coach at Michigan—was the one who was recruiting our area," Gallagher said. "I can remember he had come down to watch me play in a game, but I was dinged up that week and couldn't play. But he came and saw me play basketball—we wound up winning the district that year—and I guess he was impressed with my athletic ability on the basketball court.

"He was also good friends with Chuck Asher, and Coach Asher had told him about me and suggested he come to a basketball game. Recruiting back then wasn't like it is today; it relied a lot more on word of mouth. And if your coach told a college coach you could play, that's how it worked. I like to say I got a football scholarship by playing basketball."

Offering Gallagher a football scholarship basically sight unseen turned out to be a prescient decision for the Wolverines. While at Michigan, Gallagher played defensive tackle and helped lead the Wolverines to Big Ten titles or co-championships in 1971, 1972 and 1973. He played in the Rose Bowl in 1972 and was named a team captain as a senior in 1973. Gallagher was named an All–Big Ten selection and All-American as a senior. He racked up 83 tackles as a senior and 175 total in his final three years.

The University of Michigan's Bentley Historical Library describes Gallagher as "one of the finest defensive tackles ever to play at Michigan." In 2005, *Motown Sports Revival* named him one of the one hundred greatest players in Michigan history, ranking him number sixty-five on the all-time team.

He also continued to excel in the classroom, earning All-Academic Big Ten honors in 1971, 1972 and 1973. He was the Big Ten Medal of Honor winner in 1973. He also was a recipient of the National Football Foundation and College Football Hall of Fame postgraduate scholarship.

Following his graduation from Michigan in 1974, the Chicago Bears took Gallagher with the twentieth pick of the first round—one pick ahead of future NFL Hall of Fame receiver Lynn Swann. Gallagher was drafted ahead of five players who would go on to be inducted into the NFL Hall of Fame: Swann, tight end Dave Casper, linebacker Jack Lambert, wide receiver John Stallworth and center Mike Webster.

He was reunited with former Piqua teammate Craig Clemons on the Bears team his rookie season. He then played two seasons with the New York Giants and two seasons with the Detroit Lions.

While playing in the NFL, Gallagher attended medical school at the University of Michigan part time, eventually earning his medical degree. He currently serves as an orthopedic surgeon with Southern Indiana Orthopedics. He and his wife, Betty, reside in Columbus, Indiana, and have three children: Bryn, Patrick and Andrew.

Matt Finkes

Matt Finkes frequently talks about blue chip high school football recruits on his sports-talk radio show in Columbus. He knows that had college football recruiting been the big business in the early 1990s that it is today, he likely would not have been one of them.

"Three stars? Maybe if I was lucky," the Piqua High School graduate said of recruiting's five-star system, which ranks high school football players based on perceived college potential. "I probably would have been a two-star guy."

Despite winning nearly every imaginable award on the football field at Piqua—coupled with a standout wrestling and track career—Finkes, a 1993 Piqua graduate, was relatively lightly recruited coming out of high school, as he was viewed as an undersized defensive lineman. Former Ohio State coach John Cooper took a chance on Finkes. Finkes may not have been a "workout warrior" or possessed prototypical size for a college defensive lineman, but Cooper saw two things in Finkes that a number of major colleges may have overlooked: incredible technique and a motor that didn't quit.

At Piqua, Finkes was a dominant defensive tackle and fullback. He helped lead the Indians to Greater Miami Valley Conference titles as a sophomore and junior, three playoff appearances and trips to the Division I state semifinals as a sophomore and senior. During his time at Piqua, the Indians went 42-6.

He also racked up plenty of individual accolades. He was named first-team All-GMVC and All-Ohio as a junior and senior. He also was named Most Valuable Player at the Ohio North-South All-Star game in

THE BATTLE ON THE MIAMI

Following his career at Piqua, Matt Finkes went on to earn All-American honors at The Ohio State University. *Courtesy of The Ohio State University.*

1993 and was the team's MVP as a senior. In addition, he placed third at heavyweight in the Division I state wrestling tournament both as a junior and senior and was a state qualifier in the shot put while competing for the Piqua track team as a senior.

"Playing at Piqua helped keep me grounded, especially playing for Bill Nees," Finkes said in an interview with the *Piqua Daily Call*. "Even when he has stars such as myself or Quinn or Brandon, he has the ability to ground guys, to humble you. Even when he has great talent, he gets the most out of guys. When you play at Piqua and you play for Bill Nees, you realize you are a part of something bigger. You learn to put the team ahead of yourself.

"Why do so many superstars and five-star guys wash out in college? Because they are not used to being a part of a team concept. When you get to a place like OSU, you are just another five-star guy. It doesn't matter if you were the king of your high school. I never felt like that. I learned at Piqua to always put the team first."

That attitude carried Finkes a long way during his playing days at Ohio State. Despite his relatively unheralded status as a recruit, Finkes earned immediate playing time as a true freshman on a 1993 team that captured a share of the Big Ten title. During his playing days at Ohio State, the Buckeyes won Big Ten titles in 1993 and 1996 and captured the 1997 Rose Bowl title with a win over Arizona State. Finkes helped the Buckeyes clinch that Rose Bowl berth with a fumble return for a touchdown in a win over Indiana. Ohio State went 42-7-1 during Finkes's four years there.

Much like he did in high school, Finkes also captured numerous individual awards. He was a two-time All-American, a Freshman All-American, a three-time first-team All–Big Ten selection, the team's Bill Willis Most Valuable Defensive Lineman as a sophomore and senior, the team's Defensive MVP as a senior and a two-time Citrus Bowl Defensive MVP. Following graduation, Finkes played in the East-West Shrine Game, where he was named the game's Defensive MVP.

Finkes was taken in the fifth round of the 1997 NFL draft before being traded to the New York Jets. He played for the Jets, Washington Redskins and Jacksonville Jaguars.

He currently is a TV and radio host in Columbus, in addition to serving as associate director of development for The Ohio State University Medical Center.

Quinn Pitcock

For Bill Nees, the eyes told the entire story. "I saw Quinn walking around before the game and you could tell he had a look in his eye," Piqua's head coach said of his star defensive tackle following the Indians' 28–0 win over Troy in 2001. "I don't think Quinn felt as though he played as well as he was

THE BATTLE ON THE MIAMI

capable of playing in this game last year [a 24–14 Troy victory]. You just knew he wanted to come out and make something special happen tonight."

Pitcock did just that, continually caving in the Trojans' line of scrimmage as he led the Indians to victory. He made a habit of doing that during his playing career—particularly in two wins against Troy as a sophomore and senior.

Pitcock graduated from Piqua High School as one of the most decorated players in school history. A three-year starter, the 2002 graduate was named first-team All-Ohio twice, first-team All-Southwest District twice and first-team all-conference three times. He was the Greater Western Ohio Conference Player of the Year in 2000, won the team's Red Gabriel Award in 2000 and was named the team's 2001 Most Valuable Player and Most Valuable Defensive Lineman. As a junior, he helped lead the Indians to a spot in the Division II state title game. He also was named Outstanding Defensive Lineman in the 2001 North-South All-Star Game, was a second-team *USA Today* All-American and was rated a top 100 college prospect by the Scout.com recruiting service.

Pitcock became one of the most highly recruited players in the country, picking up offers from nearly every major Division I program in the nation. After narrowing his choices to Ohio State, Penn State and Notre Dame, Pitcock elected to play for the Buckeyes.

While there, the honors and accolades continued to roll in for Pitcock. After redshirting in 2002—Ohio State's national championship season—Pitcock immediately found himself thrown into the mix, starting for four years at defensive tackle. He won the school's Jack Stephenson Outstanding Defensive Lineman Award in 2003, the Bill Marshall Warrior Award in 2004 and the Bill Willis Outstanding Defensive Lineman Award in 2006. As a junior, he was named second-team All–Big Ten. As a senior, he was a consensus first-team All-American and first-team All–Big Ten. He was selected as a team captain and was an Academic All-American. He also was a finalist for the Ronnie Lott Trophy and the Lombardi Trophy. He helped lead the Buckeyes to the 2006 BCS National Championship game.

Following his playing days at The Ohio State University, the Indianapolis Colts took Pitcock in the third round (ninety-eighth overall) of the 2007 NFL draft. He played one season for the Colts, recording eighteen tackles and one and a half quarterback sacks. He retired following his rookie season to deal with bouts of depression and video game addiction.

Pitcock returned to football in 2010, playing in the preseason with the Seattle Seahawks and then again in the 2011 preseason with the Detroit

Lions. He played with the AFL's Orlando Predators in 2012 and 2013 before being traded to the Arizona Rattlers in early 2014.

In Arizona, Pitcock—who played in four bowl games in the state while a member of the Buckeyes—has found peace on the football field and a home within the community. After falling short in the state title game in high school and the 2006 national title game in college, Pitcock recently won a championship—to go along with the title he did win as a redshirt in 2002—with the Rattlers.

"Part of winning a championship was redemption for me," Pitcock said. "It was the biggest win, I felt like, in my career. I was able to do it with a bunch of guys who have really accepted me and taken me in as part of their family."

Brandon Saine

It was supposed to be a joke—an idea cooked up by a handful of practical jokers from Troy. Brandon Saine didn't find it particularly funny, however.

The night before the Piqua football team's game against rival Troy in 2006, a group of students broke into Piqua's Alexander Stadium/Purk Field and spray-painted a number of derogatory statements about the Indians on the grass field inside the stadium. Saine, Piqua's star running back, was a specific target of their vitriol, with the phrase "Saine is lame" spray-painted in large letters across the field.

As was so often the case during his storied career at Piqua, however, the mild-mannered Saine let his actions do the talking. The next night during the game, Saine finished with 110 rushing yards, 73 receiving yards and three touchdowns as the Indians torched the Trojans 42–7.

"I never worried too much about that stuff," Saine said of the vandalism that put him squarely in the crosshairs. "I just worried about playing football."

Something Saine did as well or better than any other player in Piqua High School history. Again, though, not that you'd know it from talking to Saine.

For Brandon Saine, playing football at Piqua High School wasn't about establishing greatness but merely about upholding the tradition of greatness that had been set long before he got there.

"The foundation was set before I got there," Saine said. "They had great players and great teams before I got there. For me, it was about carrying on that tradition. Piqua is a blue-collar town that is all about dedication. They have great

THE BATTLE ON THE MIAMI

Piqua running back Brandon Saine was named Mr. Football Ohio in 2006. He went on to play at The Ohio State University. *Courtesy of The Ohio State University.*

coaches who instill that into you. By far, that was the biggest aid to me throughout my career. I had to work hard for everything I got.

"If I had anything handed to me at Piqua, it would have been a tragedy. I wouldn't have had to have work as hard as I did—and that would have been a waste of the talents I already did have."

Those values—coupled with a blazing speed that made Saine one of the greatest sprinters in Ohio track and field history—helped propel Saine and his teammates to heights never seen at Piqua High School before or since. As a senior running back, Saine helped the 2006 Piqua football team to a Division II state championship while earning Mr. Football Ohio honors at the same time. Saine would go on to play at The Ohio State University and with the NFL's Green Bay Packers.

Honors are something Saine knows plenty about, having won more than his share in both high school and college. In addition to being named Mr. Football as a senior, Saine was a two-time first-team All-Ohio selection and a two-time Greater Western Ohio Conference Player of the Year. He also was a dominant sprinter for the Piqua track and field team, capturing four state titles and a national title in the sixty-meter dash. He still holds the Ohio Division I state record in the one-hundred-meter dash (10.38 seconds).

For the ever-humble Saine, however, his greatest accomplishment in high school was winning a state football title alongside his teammates.

"It was crazy," Saine said. "We had high expectations that year—as they do every year at Piqua. We knew we had some key guys in some positions, but we really came together as a team that year. We lost our first game, which I think kind of humbled us and showed us we still had to work together as a team. Everyone had to pull their own weight. We also lost our last regular-season game, which I think humbled us again going into the playoffs. It got us in the right state of mind—we didn't drink the Kool-Aid, so to speak.

"When I think back to that state championship, I think we learned you can't win it as an individual. I don't think I was even the best player on our team in the playoffs. We had so many guys step up and help us win that title."

Following his career at Piqua, Saine—a University of Michigan fan growing up—went on to play at The Ohio State University. He lettered for four years with the Buckeyes. In his time in Columbus, Ohio State never lost to Michigan, winning a Rose Bowl and Sugar Bowl while Saine was there.

"I did grow up wearing a Desmond Howard jersey," Saine said. "A lot of that was a product of people in my family being Michigan fans. Plus, there are so many Ohio State fans around here, so why not root for someone else? But during the recruiting process, the number-one reason I chose Ohio State was because of the relationship I had with the coaching staff. Plus, I felt like Ohio State had the highest upside for me.

"This may sound like a shot at Michigan, but they really didn't actively recruit me until I already had an offer from Ohio State. Ohio State was there first. Plus, it was also the best opportunity for my family to come see me play, with Ohio State only being an hour and a half away. And my girlfriend at the time—now my wife—was also going to school in Columbus. Really, there were a lot of reasons why I chose Ohio State."

Saine was named Ohio State's Outstanding Freshman in 2007 and Outstanding Back in 2009 and won the Warrior Award in 2010. He was Academic All–Big Ten in 2007, second-team All–Big Ten in 2009 and voted a team captain in 2010.

THE BATTLE ON THE MIAMI

Saine went undrafted out of college but signed an undrafted free agent deal with the Green Bay Packers in 2011. He played for the Packers in 2011 and 2012 before a series of injuries brought his career to a premature end. Currently, Saine works in customer development for Kimberly Clark. He and his wife, Kylie, have one son, Grey.

Chapter 11
LEGENDS OF THE FALL

Troy's Greatest Players

Bob Ferguson

A stroke took away his ability to run. Diabetes took away his legs, his eyesight and, eventually, his life.

No power on Earth, however, will take away Bob Ferguson's legacy as one of the greatest football players in Troy High School and Ohio State history.

Ferguson passed away in December 2004 at age sixty-five in Columbus after years of battling diabetes. While the man may be gone, those who saw the bullish fullback play will never forget his deeds and accomplishments.

"He was something special," Herb Hartman, a teammate of Ferguson's at Troy, said in a 2004 interview with the *Troy Daily News* following his passing. Hartman's older brother Gabe played with Ferguson both at Troy and Ohio State. "What I'll remember most is that if you didn't clear your blocks in time, you were going to get stepped on. It was just a matter of making your blocks and waiting for the locomotive to come in behind you. Then you would watch him run over people downfield."

Stories of Ferguson's punishing running style have become the stuff of legend. According to one story, a reserve sophomore defensive lineman was trying to win a spot on varsity in the mid-'50s at the expense of a senior offensive lineman who already had his spot on varsity locked down. Time after time, however, the sophomore defensive lineman was outhustling the senior, much to the upperclassman's chagrin. Rather than take matters into his own hands, however, the senior had a much better idea. "If you

THE BATTLE ON THE MIAMI

Following a stellar career at Troy, Bob Ferguson was a two-time All-American at The Ohio State University. *Courtesy of The Ohio State University.*

don't stop, it," the senior reportedly told the sophomore, "I'm not going to block you at all on the next play." The senior was true to his word, and on the very next play, he stepped aside and let the sophomore get plowed under by Ferguson.

The numbers Ferguson put up at Troy certainly back up the testaments to his greatness. For forty years, he owned nearly every rushing record in school history. In his career, Ferguson rushed for 5,521 yards, including 2,089 yards in 1956 and 1,423 in 1957. He also held the school record for points scored in a career (578).

All of those records were eventually eclipsed by Ryan Brewer in the mid-'90s. Ferguson still has the top two single-game rushing totals in school history: 529 yards against Kiser in 1956 and 475 yards against Monroe in 1956. Ferguson's rushing total against Kiser was tops in the state of Ohio until Williamsburg single-wing quarterback Jason Bainum broke it in 2001.

Around Ferguson, Troy coach Lou Juillerat built one of the most powerful squads in Troy history. From the time Ferguson was a sophomore until his graduation, the Trojans went 27-0, outscoring opponents by an average score of 31.7–9.1.

Around Troy, Ferguson became more than just a football player—and football became more than just a sport. Ferguson and the teams he played on turned Trojans from football fans into football zealots.

"Everyone got involved in it," Herb Hartman said in 2004. "It was the talk of the town."

"Oh, everybody in town loved him," said Wilma Ford, Ferguson's sister, in a 2004 interview. "It was a very exciting time, when he was playing for Troy."

Even those who never saw Ferguson play in person are well aware of his accomplishments.

"I think he's a legend not only in Troy, but throughout the state," said Steve Nolan, former Troy football coach, in 2004. "From the stories I've heard about his abilities and some of the game film I've seen of him, it was pretty obvious he was special.

"One of the first things that happened when I came to this community and people started talking football was his name was always mentioned as the elite player. When I saw his records for the first time in print, I couldn't believe them. They were that unreal—especially when you consider he was constantly the target on that offense."

After graduating from Troy High School, Ferguson went on to have an outstanding career playing for Woody Hayes at The Ohio State University. He was a two-time All-American and a two-time All–Big Ten first-team selection (1960 and '61). In 1961, he won the coveted Maxwell Trophy and finished second to Syracuse fullback Ernie Davis in one of the closest votes in Heisman Trophy history.

He finished his career at OSU with 2,162 rushing yards, the fourteenth highest total in school history. He often saved his best games for rival Michigan. The Buckeyes went 3-1 against the Wolverines in his four years in Columbus. As a senior, Ferguson rushed for four touchdowns as the Buckeyes rolled to a 50–20 win over Michigan in 1961.

Ferguson was the perfect fit in Hayes's "three yards and a cloud of dust" offense. In three years as an Ohio State starter, Ferguson was never once tackled behind the line of scrimmage—an almost unheard-of feat. Hayes once called Ferguson "the greatest fullback I've had at Ohio State." Ferguson was elected to the College Football Hall of Fame in 1995.

Following graduation, Ferguson was a first-round draft pick by both the San Diego Chargers (AFL) and the Pittsburgh Steelers (NFL). A series of injuries cut Ferguson's NFL career short before it ever got started, however. He bounced around to a number of teams before retiring.

Following his retirement, Ferguson was a social worker in Columbus. In 1991, he suffered a massive stroke. He spent much of his final years battling the effects of the stroke and diabetes.

"I'm glad he got one last Christmas with his wife and his kids and his grandkids," Ford said. "I know that meant a lot to him. They meant a lot to him, and he meant a lot to them. They'll never forget him. I don't think anyone who knew Bob will ever forget him."

TOM MYERS

While playing quarterback at Troy High School, Tom Myers put together more highlights than few ever had before or have since. It's not the wins he led his team to or the records he piled up that Myers most remembers, however. In fact, the moment that sticks with him the most was one of the lowest points of his career.

"Unfortunately, while I had many positive experiences at Troy, the one that really sticks out is my sophomore year when we lost [14–0 in 1958] to Fairmont and ended Troy's thirty-two-game winning streak," Myers said. "Coach [Lou] Juillerat was the best. He pulled me aside and let me know I hadn't played well. I knew I had a dismal game."

That loss served as a touchstone moment in Myers's legendary career. It lit a spark under him that carried him to unprecedented heights in Troy history and All-America honors at Northwestern.

"That really lit a fire under me," Myers said. "I knew I could do better. I think that was a turning point in my career. Now I look at it as a positive thing. Coach understood what he needed to do. I respected him a lot and worshipped every word he said."

Myers would have few down moments after that game in 1958. He would go on to set every passing record in school history—nearly all of which still stand more than five decades later. While other records have fallen over the years, Myers's still stand strong. He still holds the top two records for most passing yards in a game (376 in a 74–0 win over Belmont in 1959 and 351 in a 78–0 win over Miamisburg that same year), the top marks for passing yards in a season (2,009 in 1960 and 1,963 in 1959) and the top spot for most passing yards in a career (5,060).

Myers also holds school records for passing touchdowns in a game (five touchdown passes, which he did four times in his career: against Belmont in 1959, in a 58–0 win over Stivers in 1960, in a 62–0 win over rival Piqua in 1960 and in a 52–0 win over Xenia in 1960), most touchdown passes in a season (twenty-eight in 1960 and twenty-one in 1959) and touchdown passes in a career (sixty-one).

"I do think that's amazing," Myers said of still holding every school passing record. "I don't want to sound critical, but records were made to be broken. But with Coach Juillerat, we ran a pretty wide-open offense. We ran shotgun and spread before a lot of college or pro teams were doing that. We really were pretty ahead of our time."

Following a career that saw him earn All-Ohio honors at Troy, Myers went on to play at Northwestern, where he wasted little time in making an impact. Playing for Coach Ara Parseghian, Myers earned the starting nod against South Carolina as a nineteen-year-old sophomore. He promptly completed the first fifteen passes he threw, setting an NCAA record. The Wildcats got off to a 6-0 start and were, at one point in the season, the top-ranked team in the country. The Wildcats would finish the season 7-2. Myers was named an All-American following that season.

Myers would play two seasons in the NFL with the Detroit Lions.

Myers currently lives in North Carolina but says he still has friends and family who live in the area—including "a brother who lives in that town a few miles up the road whose name we don't say out loud"—and he gets back to Troy several times per year.

Tom Vaughn

It doesn't take long for Tom Vaughn to figure out what hurts when he wakes up every morning. "I hurt everywhere," Vaughn said from his home in Arizona. "When I wake up, everything hurts and I thank God I am still alive. I'm one of those old guys who has to put ointment on everything."

Such are the remnants of a football career that was as legendary—or, in most cases, more legendary—than any other player in Troy High School history.

THE BATTLE ON THE MIAMI

Troy's Tommy Vaughn was an All-American at Iowa State University. *Courtesy of Iowa State University.*

Vaughn—along with classmate and former Trojan quarterback Tom Myers—left his name scrawled all over the Troy High School record books. While most other records have been surpassed since the two graduated in 1961, the surnames Vaughn and Myers still remain atop nearly every receiving and passing record at Troy.

Vaughn still holds the top two spots for receiving yards in a season (703 in 1959 and 627 in 1960), the record for most receiving yards in a career (1,451), touchdown receptions in a game (four), touchdown receptions in a season (thirteen) and touchdown receptions in a career (twenty-five). Perhaps the most versatile football player in school history, Vaughn also twice rushed for more than 1,000 yards in a season (1,130 in 1959 and 1,117 in 1960). He also holds the record for most points scored in a game (48 in a 78–18 win over Sidney in 1960), is third on the list for points scored in a season (230 in 1960) and is third for most points scored in a career (514).

All of which he credits to his teammates and coaches.

"To set records like that, you first have to have an outstanding offensive line, you have to have an outstanding quarterback to throw you the ball and you've got to have a coach that has the confidence in you to get the job done," Vaughn said. "I had all of those things. My offensive line always told me, 'We'll block for you—all you have to do is catch the ball.' I loved my offensive line. I loved all my teammates. We were all very concentrated and all focused."

There may also have been another secret to Vaughn's success: Troy's offense touched the ball more than most.

"A lot of people don't know this, but our coach, Lou Juillerat, went for an onside kick every time we scored," Vaughn said. "We never once kicked the ball deep after we scored a touchdown. If the other team recovered it, we didn't care. We had so much confidence that our defense could stop them, we let them have the ball at the forty. We didn't care."

Following his star-studded career at Troy, Vaughn went on to play at Iowa State University, where the accolades kept rolling in. One of the last great two-way players in college football history, Vaughn—who played running back and defensive back—was named first team All–Big Eight Conference on both offense and defense in 1963. In 1964, he earned All–Big Eight and All-America honors. In 1965, he was named Iowa State Athlete of the Year. In 2005, he was inducted into Iowa State's Hall of Fame.

Following his graduation from Iowa State, Vaughn was drafted in the fifth round of the 1965 NFL draft by the Detroit Lions. He enjoyed a successful seven-year career with the Lions, earning the starting position at strong safety in 1967. Along with Lem Barney, Dick LeBeau and Mike Weger, Vaughn would help form one of the NFL's best pass defenses during the late 1960s.

He still ranks in the Lions' top ten in both kickoff and punt returns, and he intercepted nine passes in his career. In a poll published in 2003, he was voted as one of the top one hundred players in Detroit Lions history.

Max Urick

Athletics have taken Max Urick across the country and around the world and allowed him to hold some of the most prestigious jobs in the world of sports. And it all started in Troy.

THE BATTLE ON THE MIAMI

"Athletics have always played a big role in my life," Urick said. "I can remember when I was a kid going down to meet my dad at Hobart Manufacturing. I'd be walking along with one of my friends, and I might pick up a stone and say, 'Let's see who can hit that telephone pole.' I remember having tricycle races when I was a kid.

"I'm a big believer in the value of amateur sports and what sports can do for people. Sports certainly has played a meaningful role in my life, and it all started in Troy. From friends to coaches to teachers to music to art to sports, anything the high school did contributed to the lives of students."

Urick took what he learned from his time in Troy and applied it on the playing field, on the sidelines and in athletic administration positions.

Urick started his career in athletics as a fierce player on some of the greatest football teams in school history. Nicknamed the "Baby-faced Assassin," he earned first-team All-Ohio honors as a center and linebacker in 1955. He went on to play football, wrestle and play lacrosse at Ohio Wesleyan University. He was an All-America center and linebacker in football, a conference wrestling champion and an All-America in lacrosse—a sport he had never played before attending college.

"Back then, I lived my life from one season to the next," Urick said. "We didn't have spring football at Ohio Wesleyan, but I knew I had to have that structure that athletics provided. The lacrosse program had just started as a varsity sport, and I was attracted to the physical nature of it. It's something I just picked up in college. It's really a great sport and is growing now in popularity."

Following his decorated athletic career, Urick went into coaching upon graduation. He was an assistant football coach at Army in 1962, an assistant coach at The Ohio State University from 1963 to 1966, the head coach at Wabash College from 1967 to 1990 and an assistant coach at Duke University from 1971 to 1973.

Following his coaching career, Urick would again return to athletics in 1983, taking over as athletic director in 1983 and staying until 1993, when he took over as athletic director at Kansas State University. He would remain in that position until his retirement in 2001.

Sometimes as a coach and administrator, Urick would draw on the lessons he learned while playing football at Troy. One memory from his storied career sticks out in particular. "I'll never forget one game we were going to and we were all on the bus waiting," he said. "[Fellow Trojan Athletics Hall of Fame inductee and two-time Ohio State All-American] Bob Ferguson was late. Coach [Lou] Juillerat said, 'Let's go!' and we left without him. We were all pretty anxious; we couldn't believe we were leaving without Bob Ferguson. As it turned out, his dad had driven him to the game and he met us down there, but that left an indelible impression on me—you don't be late. If Coach Juillerat told you to be somewhere, you had better be there five minutes early.

"I don't know that I did that specifically as a coach or administrator, but I did learn something—you don't make exceptions for anybody. Everyone is expected to pull the load. I don't know that I consciously used that, but I guess you could say it was one of those moments of enlightenment. Now it all makes sense, and it helped me and served me well in my career."

Gordon Bell

More than forty years after the fact, Gordon Bell would like to confirm that the legend surrounding his graduation from Troy High School is not just a piece of lore forever woven into the rich tapestry of Troy High School football and told time and again for four decades, but the God's-honest truth.

When Bell—a star running back at Troy in the early 1970s—graduated, Chuck Asher, the former coach at rival Piqua High School, offered to present Bell with his diploma at Troy's commencement ceremonies.

"It's a true story," Bell said. "When I graduated, he was so glad to see me go he offered to come down and give me my diploma. He was happy he wouldn't have to see me anymore. He was tired of seeing me play against Piqua."

It's hard to blame Asher. Bell tortured the Indians for three years on varsity, right from the very start.

In the first game of the season in 1969, Troy played its rival. The Indians—who featured future NFL defensive lineman Dave Gallagher—came in heavily favored against the Trojans, who had gone just 2-8 the year before. On the first play from scrimmage, Bell—then an unknown sophomore tailback who had never played a down on varsity—ripped off a sixty-eight-yard touchdown run as the Trojans went on to stun the Indians, 22–6.

"Playing against Piqua were probably the moments from high school I'll remember most," Bell said. "It was always kind of special. My sophomore year, I scored a touchdown on the first play of the game. My junior year, I scored a touchdown on the second play of the game. My senior year, I scored a touchdown on the first play of the game."

THE BATTLE ON THE MIAMI

At least Piqua can take solace in this—it wasn't alone. During his career at Troy, Bell made nearly every opponent he took on look bad. His stellar career is a big reason why he'll be inducted as a member of the inaugural class of the Trojan Athletics Hall of Fame.

Bell graduated from Troy as one of the most decorated players in school history. His name still is written all over the school record books. He's fourth in school history in career rushing yards (3,707), fifth in points scored in a career (340), eleventh in points scored in a season (146) and has the sixth-highest single-game rushing total in school history (324 yards in a 54–6 win over Piqua in 1970). He was a two-time first-team All-Ohio selection at running back and, in 1971, was runner-up to future two-time Heisman Trophy winner Archie Griffin for Associated Press Back of the Year honors.

Perhaps as impressive, Bell helped lead the Trojans to back-to-back 10-0 seasons on teams that were generally regarded as some of the best in the state in an era that preceded a playoff system.

Following his standout career at Troy, Bell went on to the University of Michigan. In 1974, he rushed for 1,048 yards despite starting just three games. In 1975, he led the Big Ten in rushing with 1,390 yards—more than Griffin, who won the Heisman at Ohio State that season—was named first-

Following his career at Troy, Gordon Bell won All-American honors at the University of Michigan. *Courtesy of the University of Michigan.*

team All–Big Ten and was an AP All-American. That year, Bell set single-season school records for all-purpose yards (1,714), most 100-yard rushing games (eight) and most rushing attempts (273).

Following his career at Michigan, Bell played in the NFL for three seasons with the New York Giants and St. Louis Cardinals.

Randy Walker

John Terwilliger just wanted to go home. Randy Walker had other ideas, however.

It was 1971, and Terwilliger—then an assistant football coach at Troy High School—had just supervised one of the Trojans' team workouts. Before he could lock up and go home, however, he had to clear out the weight room—not an easy task when Walker was in there.

"He was a kid that kept you there," Terwilliger said in a June 2006 *Troy Daily News* interview just days after Walker—a Troy High School graduate and the former Northwestern University coach—died of a heart attack at age fifty-two. "When you wanted to go home, he was the kid who said, 'C'mon, let me see if I can do this one more time.' That's just the type of kid he was.

"As a coach, you want to impact the lives of young people and make an impression on them. Randy was the reverse of that. When all was said and done, he impacted the coaches as much as we impacted him. He was just a very honest, very hard-working kid."

It was that type of work ethic and dedication that made Walker a star at every level of football he participated in—from his playing days at Troy and Miami University through his college coaching stops at Miami and, finally, Northwestern University.

Those who knew him at Troy remember Walker as a tireless worker who never settled for anything less than perfection from himself, his teammates and the players he coached.

"When we first started the weightlifting program, there were three levels you could attain, based on the standards you were able to achieve," said Troy resident and former teammate Tim Pierce in a June 2006 interview following Walker's death. "There was the Trojan Club, the Sam Huff Club—one of our coaches, Barry Blackstone, was a big Sam Huff and West Virginia fan—and the Helmet Club. A lot of us made the Trojan

THE BATTLE ON THE MIAMI

Club. Some of us made the Sam Huff Club. Randy was the one person who made the Helmet Club. He was the only one. It was just something that he set his mind toward doing—he wanted to attain all the standards he needed to make that club. Really, it's pretty impressive, considering some of the guys we had in that club—guys like [Dave] Starkey and Gordon Bell."

Pierce remembers that drive taking Walker a long way—probably further than his natural ability would have dictated. "He almost got cut in junior high," Pierce said. "He was kind of short and fat. But he worked harder than anybody else. I know whenever he talked to kids, that's something he always made sure he told them—if they worked hard, good things would happen. Just look at him."

Walker went from being almost cut in junior high to being a star for the Troy powerhouses of the early '70s. The Trojans went undefeated his junior and senior seasons and—in an era that preceded postseason play—were generally regarded as one of the top teams in the state.

After graduating from Troy, Walker took his considerable football talents to Miami University. By his senior season at Miami, Walker—who played three different positions for the Redskins (now RedHawks) that year—earned team MVP honors and was an All-Mid-American Conference second-team running back selection. For his career, Walker rushed for 1,757 yards on 417 carries, then the sixth highest total in school history.

He was drafted in the thirteenth round of the NFL draft by the Cincinnati Bengals and played sparingly in the preseason. It was after he returned to Miami as a graduate assistant coach that his coaching career began to flourish.

After his first stop at Miami, he took assistant positions at North Carolina and Northwestern from 1977 to 1989. In 1990, he became head coach at his alma mater, a position he would hold until 1998. During his time with the RedHawks, Walker compiled a record of 59-35-5 (.621), a mark that made him the winningest coach in school history.

In 1999, Walker was named head coach at Northwestern. He was the first Northwestern coach to lead the school to three bowl games. His Wildcats won thirty-seven games, going 7-5 in his final season. Northwestern shared the Big Ten title in 2000 and went to the Alamo Bowl. The Wildcats also went to the 2003 Motor City Bowl.

OHIO'S TROY VS. PIQUA FOOTBALL RIVALRY

Ryan Brewer

Say this for Ryan Brewer—he doesn't take slights lightly.

Just ask former Ohio State football coach John Cooper. Or the Piqua football team.

When asked to pick one moment that he'll most remember from a career with the Troy High School football team that earned him a spot in the inaugural Trojan Athletics Hall of Fame, Brewer didn't select any of his record-breaking moments, earning Mr. Football Ohio or appearing in *Sports Illustrated*. He selected the time he was burned in effigy at a Piqua pep rally before the annual showdown with Troy.

"I remember the time they burned a dummy of me at the Piqua bonfire," Brewer said. "I'll never forget that."

In the game between the two bitter rivals the next night, Brewer rushed for more than two hundred yards as the Trojans triumphed—the fourth time in a row they did that in Brewer's career against the Indians.

"I still remember the picture in the paper," Brewer said of one particular run during the game. "I had the ball on a sweep, and some guy from Piqua got a hand on me—think it was no. 6. I gave him a stiff arm and broke free. His neck probably still hurts from that. At least I hope it does."

The lesson is simple: you may "burn" Ryan Brewer once, but chances are he is going to get the last laugh.

It's a lesson Cooper had to learn the hard way. Despite rushing for 2,856 yards in ten games his senior season in 1998 and being named the top football player in the state, Brewer never received a scholarship offer from Cooper and the Buckeyes. Not that Ohio State was alone; none of the Big Ten schools or other Midwest powers came up with scholarship offers for Brewer, whom many recruiting analysts deemed too small and too slow to play at the Division I level.

Brewer instead opted for a scholarship offer from South Carolina, which was in the midst of one of the worst losing streaks in school history at the time. Under the guidance of Coach Lou Holtz, the Gamecocks quickly turned things around, earning a trip to the Outback Bowl Brewer's sophomore season.

South Carolina's opponent in that bowl game?

Ohio State.

Once again, Brewer cashed in on his chance for revenge as he tallied 214 all-purpose yards and scored three touchdowns to lead the Gamecocks to a 24–7 victory over the Buckeyes. In the game's aftermath, Brewer was named the game's MVP, and Cooper was fired as Ohio State's head coach the very next day.

"I have a lot of great memories from Troy—but that Ohio State game in the Outback Bowl is tough to top," Brewer said.

Indeed, Brewer's accomplishments in his four years at Troy are seemingly endless. He holds nearly every major rushing record in school history, including career rushing yards (7,656), single-season rushing yards (2,856), most points scored in a season (288) and most points scored in a career (761). Not only are his totals school records, but they are also seemingly untouchable. He's the only running back to rush for more than 2,000 yards in a season twice in his career, and his career rushing total is more than 2,100 yards more than the second-best total in school history.

"It was a heck of a ride growing up in Troy," Brewer said. "From the school itself to the coaching staff to the teachers to my teammates, I don't think I would want it any other way. If you are a big-time high school football fan, Troy is the best place in the world to be."

Following his career at South Carolina, Brewer played briefly in NFL Europe before returning to South Carolina and opening his own business. While he's gone on to a successful career after football, Brewer said he'll never forget his time at Troy.

"It's pretty special," he said.

Kris Dielman

When asked to pick a favorite moment from his high school football career, Kris Dielman has hundreds to choose from. He could have picked any one of his individual moments of glory—the helmet-cracking hits, the pancake blocks or the touchdown catches. True to form, however, Dielman didn't go that route.

"My favorite memory is probably just winning games," Dielman said. "More than anything, that's what I'll remember. In high school, I just thought you were supposed to win football games—it seemed like we always won football games. Lo and behold, then I go to Indiana and we never won football games. Heck, we only lost four games the entire time I was at Troy.

"Those were some of the most fun and special moments of my life—being in the locker room after a game with the music blaring after you just beat the [heck] out of somebody and celebrating with my teammates. It's not easy winning football games at any level—high school, college or pro. You've got to put in a lot of work. But it's all worth it when you win."

That Dielman would select a team moment rather than an individual moment during his career at Troy probably comes as no surprise to anyone who watched him play. One of the most selfless—and intense—players in school history, Dielman made a habit of putting the team first when he played at Troy, Indiana University and for the NFL's San Diego Chargers.

He started his football career at Troy at tight end. In Troy's run-heavy offense, he didn't get a chance to catch many passes but still made a name for himself as a sophomore and junior as one of the most devastating blockers in school history. His senior year—with the Trojans sitting on an 0-2 record after going 20-0 the previous two regular seasons—Dielman started playing middle linebacker in addition to tight end.

His impact was immediately felt, as the Trojans went 8-0 to finish the season with him solidifying the defense. Dielman earned second-team All-Ohio honors for his play at middle linebacker that season.

Following high school, Dielman went to Indiana, where he played tight end his first two seasons, earning All–Big Ten honors as a junior. His junior season, the team had a need at defensive tackle, so Dielman played primarily at defensive end and continued to moonlight at tight end, becoming one of the only two-way players in Division I college football. He again earned All–Big Ten honors his senior season.

After his college career, Dielman went undrafted but signed as a free agent with the Chargers. He was eventually moved to offensive guard, a position he had never played in his career. Despite his inexperience, Dielman excelled, quickly earning a starting role. In his NFL career, he would earn five trips to the Pro Bowl and be selected to the Chargers' 50th Anniversary Team.

"It all started in little Troy, Ohio," Dielman said. "Troy will always be where my roots are. I had some of the best times of my life playing high school football."

TROY VS. PIQUA SCORES

1899	Troy 17, Piqua 0	1918	Troy 28, Piqua 6
	Troy 7, Piqua 5		Piqua 13, Troy 6
1900	Troy 2, Piqua 0	1919	Troy 21, Piqua 9
	Piqua 26, Troy 0		Piqua 19, Troy 6
	Troy 16, Piqua 0	1920	Troy 7, Piqua 6
1901	Piqua 13, Troy 8		Troy 19, Piqua 0
	Piqua 21, Troy 0	1921	Piqua 21, Troy 0
1902	Piqua 23, Troy 6		Troy 13, Piqua 2
1903	Piqua 17, Troy 0	1922	Troy 13, Piqua 0
1909	Troy 17, Piqua 5		Piqua 7, Troy 6
	Piqua 5, Troy 0	1923	Piqua 6, Troy 6
1911	Troy 5, Piqua 0		Troy 14, Piqua 6
	Piqua 0, Troy 0	1924	Piqua 7, Troy 6
1912	Piqua 32, Troy 12		Piqua 14, Troy 6
	Piqua 7, Troy 6	1925	Piqua 20, Troy 6
1913	Troy 18, Piqua 0	1926	Piqua 25, Troy 0
	Troy 85, Piqua 0	1927	Piqua 13, Troy 0
1914	Troy 20, Piqua 6	1928	Troy 13, Piqua 0
	Troy 14, Piqua 6	1929	Piqua 21, Troy 6
1915	Piqua 13, Troy 7	1930	Piqua 20, Troy 0
	Piqua 27, Troy 0	1931	Piqua 13, Troy 12
1916	Troy 13, Piqua 3	1932	Piqua 9, Troy 6
	Piqua 0, Troy 0	1933	Troy 13, Piqua 0
1917	Piqua 66, Troy 0	1934	Piqua 27, Troy 6
	Piqua 61, Troy 0	1935	Piqua 0, Troy 0

TROY VS. PIQUA SCORES

1936	Piqua 17, Troy 6	1976	Troy 27, Piqua 6
1937	Piqua 18, Troy 12	1977	Troy 16, Piqua 6
1938	Piqua 6, Troy 0	1978	Troy 26, Piqua 8
1939	Troy 6, Piqua 0	1979	Troy 28, Piqua 8
1940	Piqua 20, Troy 0	1980	Troy 35, Piqua 8
1941	Piqua 13, Troy 7	1981	Troy 26, Piqua 0
1942	Piqua 7, Troy 7	1982	Piqua 27, Troy 18
1943	Piqua 26, Troy 12	1983	Piqua 9, Troy 6
1944	Troy 20, Piqua 6	1984	Troy 47, Piqua 20
1945	Piqua 25, Troy 6	1985	Troy 26, Piqua 17
1946	Troy 12, Piqua 6	1986	Troy 28, Piqua 24
1947	Piqua 40, Troy 6	1987	Piqua 24, Troy 15
1948	Piqua 0, Troy 0	1988	Troy 39, Piqua 6
1949	Troy 20, Piqua 3	1989	Troy 17, Piqua 14
1950	Piqua 39, Troy 12	1990	Piqua 20, Troy 7
1951	Troy 41, Piqua 12	1991	Piqua 24, Troy 6
1952	Piqua 25, Troy 12	1992	Troy 22, Piqua 7
1953	Piqua 6, Troy 0		Piqua 20, Troy 7
1954	Troy 18, Piqua 0	1993	Piqua 16, Troy 15
1955	Troy 48, Piqua 0	1994	Piqua 16, Troy 13
1956	Troy 44, Piqua 6	1995	Troy 17, Piqua 14 OT
1957	Troy 41, Piqua 6	1996	Troy 48, Piqua 0
1958	Piqua 14, Troy 6	1997	Troy 28, Piqua 10
1959	Troy 20, Piqua 0	1998	Troy 31, Piqua 14
1960	Troy 62, Piqua 0	1999	Piqua 30, Troy 25
1961	Troy 12, Piqua 6	2000	Troy 24, Piqua 7
1962	Troy 20, Piqua 16	2001	Piqua 28, Troy 0
1963	Troy 28, Piqua 26	2002	Piqua 9, Troy 6
1964	Piqua 20, Troy 0	2003	Piqua 10, Troy 3
1965	Piqua 28, Troy 16	2004	Troy 30, Piqua 7
1966	Piqua 8, Troy 6	2005	Piqua 13, Troy 12
1967	Piqua 34, Troy 6	2006	Piqua 42, Troy 7
1968	Piqua 38, Troy 20	2007	Troy 36, Piqua 35
1969	Troy 22, Piqua 6	2008	Troy 49, Piqua 28
1970	Troy 54, Piqua 6	2009	Troy 26, Piqua 0
1971	Troy 36, Piqua 6	2010	Troy 27, Piqua 14
1972	Troy 26, Piqua 7	2011	Troy 27, Piqua 7
1973	Piqua 12, Troy 7	2012	Piqua 14, Troy 0
1974	Troy 34, Piqua 6	2013	Piqua 33, Troy 27
1975	Piqua 9, Troy 0	2014	Piqua 41, Troy 10

Series Totals: Troy 62, Piqua 62, Ties 6

INDEX

A

AFL 33, 36, 118, 125
Alexander Stadium 31, 92, 118
Ali, Muhammad 56
All-American 35, 36, 37, 39, 41, 51, 57, 59, 62, 90, 111, 112, 113, 116, 117, 124, 126, 129, 132
All–Big Ten 41, 111, 113, 116, 120, 124, 132, 136
Allen, Edward 20, 41, 42, 92
Allen, Matt 97
Amos Alonzo Stagg Bowl 58
Apple, John 51
Arizona Rattlers 118
Arizona State University 116
Armstrong, Brad 98
Asher, Chuck 37, 38, 39, 40, 42, 43, 44, 45, 46, 54, 111, 113, 130

B

Bainum, Jason 124
Baker, Adam 76
Baker, Alex 94
Baldwin-Wallace University 33, 58
Barr, Tom 64, 66
Bell, Gordon 12, 40, 41, 42, 43, 130, 131, 132, 133
Beougher, Ryan 65, 69, 70, 71
Bickel, Jack 34
Big Ten 111, 113, 116, 120, 133, 136
Big Ten Medal of Honor 113
Bird, Larry 56
Blackstone, Barry 45, 132
Blizman, Kevin 46
Block, William 86
Bolton, Bill 28
Bornhorst, Adam 89
Boston College 50
Bowling Green 41
Boyd, Cody 90
Boyd, Elmo 41, 90

Brading, Joe 94
Breedlove, Randy 69
Brewer, Ryan 12, 59, 66, 73, 77, 79, 81, 82, 123, 134, 135
Brewer, Scot 62, 64, 75, 76, 79, 103
Brookhaven 54
Brown, Corey 12, 13, 94, 97, 98
Buckeyes 116, 117, 118, 120, 124, 134
Buecker, Scott 65
Burgbacher, Matt 103
Bush, A.J. 90
Butsch, Steve 51, 52
Byrer, Rob 89

C

Cade, Joel 70
Calloway, Tom 27
Canadian Football League 58
Canter, Todd 51, 52
Carnes, Dick 31, 87, 89
Casper, Dave 114
Cermak, Mark 90

INDEX

Chargers' 50th Anniversary Team 136
Chicago Bears 37, 39, 110, 113
Cincinnati Anderson 78, 79, 80
Cincinnati Bengals 41, 133
Cincinnati Moeller 53
Cincinnati Princeton 54
Cincinnati Reds 30
Clarion University 57
Clay, Brad 62, 64, 66, 75
Clemons, Craig 39, 41, 51, 52, 110, 111, 112, 114
Cleveland Browns 41
Collier, Phil 92
Columbus Brookhaven 54
Conard, Jim 40, 41, 42, 43, 44, 45
Conneaut High School 47, 57
Cooper, John 114, 134
Cruse, Todd 51
Cummins, Keith 38
Current, Jake 12, 94
Custer, Ryan 90

D

Dallman, Matt 79, 80, 81, 82
Darner, Kevin 80
Davis, Ben 92
Davis, Ernie 124
Delwiche, Mike 49, 50, 51, 52
Denlinger, Todd 90
Denver Broncos 36
Detroit Lions 36, 114, 118, 126, 128
Dielman, Kris 73, 81, 82, 135, 136

Dillow, Chad 62, 64, 65, 66
Division I 32, 49, 53, 54, 59, 61, 68, 77, 79, 81, 82, 86, 88, 91, 92, 114, 115, 117, 120, 134, 136
Division II 11, 60, 77, 78, 85, 86, 88, 93, 117, 119
Dodson, Brooks 65, 69, 70, 71
Duke University 112, 129
Dunaway, Ian 98
Dunn, Brian 81

E

Eastern Kentucky University 41
Erwin, Brad 87
Evilsizor, Mark 62, 64, 65

F

Fairmont 63, 125
Favorite, Bussie 31
Ferguson, Bob 12, 33, 34, 35, 36, 82, 110, 122, 123, 124, 125, 129
Finkes, Matt 56, 59, 62, 65, 67, 70, 73, 114, 115, 116
Fobian, Shane 62
Ford, Wilma 124, 125
Foster, Marcus 82, 86, 87, 88, 98
Franklin 77
Frazier, Joe 56
Funderburg, Chad 51

G

Gallagher, Dave 37, 39, 41, 42, 43, 112, 113, 114, 130

"Game of the Century" 28, 29, 30, 61, 65
Garby Gymnasium 86
Garfield, Bill 62
General McLane High School 57
Giangulio, Larry 52
"Golden Age" 16, 46, 55, 71, 72
Goldner, Mark 38
Graham High School 58
Greater Miami Valley Conference 50, 53, 67, 73, 77, 78, 80, 88, 114
Green Bay Packers 41, 119
Greenville 63, 66, 88
Gregory, Shawn 81
Griffey, Ken, Jr. 53
Griffin, Archie 131
Grove City 54
Grump, Kevin 45, 46

H

Hartman, Gabe 35, 122
Hartman, Herb 122, 124
Hayes, Woody 33, 124
Heisman 33, 35, 124, 131
Hemm, Justin 91, 92, 94
Hobart Arena 30
Hobart family 30
Holtz, Lou 134
Honeycutt, Ryan 75, 76, 78
Hudson, Joey 89
Huff, Sam 132
Hulme, Ryan 65, 70

I

Indiana University 76, 82, 116, 135, 136
Iowa State University 34, 36, 128

INDEX

J

Jackson, Chris 81
Jacksonville Jaguars 116
Johns, Kevin 65, 66, 67, 69, 70, 75, 76
Johnson, Aaron 49, 52, 53
Johnson, Magic 56
Jones, Antwon 59, 73
Jones, David 43, 74
Jones, Zach 98
Juillerat, Lou 15, 31, 33, 34, 35, 36, 39, 40, 124, 125, 126, 128, 129

K

Kansas State University 34, 129
Karn, Ryan 80, 89
Kazmaier, Carlton 28
Keller, Keith 51
Kennedy, Patrick 21

L

Lady Justice 20
Lambert, Jack 114
Lavey, Eric 63
Lavy, Matt 51
Lee, Charles 54
Lemon Monroe 77
Levorchick, Dave 86, 87
Lillicrap, Rob 80
Lima Central Catholic High School 58
Lohrer, Mike 50
Lollis Hotel 20
Lord, Steve 51
Loveland 88
Lucas, Travis 81
Lyman, Jeff 51
Lyman, Tom 38, 51, 54, 74, 75, 76, 78, 80

M

Magoteaux, Bryan 55, 75, 76
Magoteaux, Ken 55, 62
Magoteaux, Kyle 55
Magoteaux, Steve 47, 48, 52, 53, 54, 55, 58, 62, 64, 65, 66, 67, 69, 71, 78
Manson, Jason 59, 79, 81
Marietta College 36, 40
Marshall University 41
Marysville 88
Maxwell Trophy 33, 124
May, Cody 98
Mayer, Al 41
McGillvary, Benson 11, 13, 17, 97
Mescher, Kevin 49, 53
Messer, Dustin 90
Miami County 16, 19, 20, 30, 61, 84
Miami County Courthouse 19, 20
Miami RedHawks 133
Miami Redskins 133
Miamisburg 88, 126
Miami Shores Golf Course 30
Miami Union 22
Miami University 41, 74, 132, 133
Miami Valley League 25, 26, 30, 42, 111, 112
Miami Valley Sunday News 50
Michigan State University 13
Midway Park 20, 22, 29
Miller, Jack 26, 27
Mitchell, Sean 54
Moeller, Gary 113
Montreal Alouettes 58

Mr. Football Ohio 11, 59, 82, 90, 119, 134
Mumma, John 45
Musselman, Ryan 12, 94
Myers, Tom 35, 36, 110, 125, 126, 127

N

Naegele, Dirk 51
Naval Academy 49
NBA 56
NCAA 56
Nees, Bill 16, 25, 47, 55, 56, 57, 58, 59, 60, 62, 66, 67, 68, 69, 70, 71, 72, 73, 74, 83, 86, 92, 115, 116
Neuenschwander, Ethan 54
New York Giants 37, 41, 114, 132
New York Jets 116
NFL 17, 32, 36, 37, 41, 73, 110, 112, 113, 114, 116, 117, 119, 125, 126, 128, 130, 132, 135, 136
Nolan, Steve 13, 16, 47, 48, 49, 50, 51, 52, 55, 56, 57, 58, 59, 60, 62, 64, 66, 68, 69, 72, 73, 75, 76, 77, 79, 81, 83, 87, 97, 103, 124
North Carolina 35, 50, 126
Northmont 53, 66, 67, 88
Northwestern University 36, 41, 112, 125, 126, 132, 133

INDEX

O

Ohio High School Athletic Association 44, 60
Ohio State University, The 11, 24, 33, 35, 41, 57, 59, 60, 62, 65, 90, 114, 116, 117, 119, 120, 122, 124, 129, 131, 134, 135
Ohio Wesleyan University 34, 129
Olden, Jesse 52
Orlando Predators 118
Ostendorf, Mike 38
Ouhl, Troy 54
Outback Bowl 134, 135
Oxford Talawanda 88

P

Pearson, Dick 39
Pearson, John 82, 87, 88, 111
Pierce, Tim 44, 45, 132, 133
Piqua Daily Call 22, 37, 39, 71, 115
Piqua High School 56, 110, 112, 114, 117, 118, 119, 130
Piqua High School Athletic Hall of Fame 111
Pitcock, Jafe 92
Pitcock, Quinn 59, 87, 88, 90, 116, 117, 118
pole vault 51
Pro Bowl 136
Purdy, Captain 28
Purk Field 31, 118

R

Richards, Allen 40, 41
Rohrbach, Scott 82, 83
Rolf, David 13, 92
Rolf, Pete 90, 92
Roosevelt Field 27
Roosevelt, Theodore 22, 23
Rose Bowl 113, 116, 120
Rose, Charles 52

S

Saine, Brandon 11, 59, 90, 93, 118, 119, 120, 121
San Diego Chargers 82, 125, 136
San Francisco 49ers 41
Schembechler, Bo 112
Scout.com 117
Shaw, Daniel 94
Shepard, Brian 64
Shilt, Alex 64, 66
Shook, Rob 64, 65, 69
Shoup, Roger 38
Sidney 11, 20, 66, 67, 127
Smith, Bill 46
Snyder, Dusty 89, 92
South Carolina 82, 126
Spencer, Jeanne 29
Sports Illustrated 134
Springfield North 63, 68, 79
Springfield South 62, 80
Stafford, Winfred 74, 78
Stallworth, John 114
Stanford 49
Starkey, Dave 41, 133
Steinke, Gene 66, 75
St. Louis Cardinals 41
Stockman, Dave 35
Stoltz, Ashlin 98
Sugar Bowl 120
Summers, John 24, 46, 87
Swann, Lynn 113

T

Terando, Kyle 98
Terwilliger, John 132
Toledo Central Catholic 53, 93
Toledo Libby 63
Toledo Rogers 79
Toledo St. Francis 68, 80
Tommy Guns, the 35
Trostle, Nick 79, 80
Trotwood-Madison 66, 67
Troy Daily News 11, 26, 29, 30, 34, 37, 38, 42, 45, 51, 63, 64, 65, 70, 79, 122, 132
Troy High School 22, 32, 33, 36, 41, 103, 110, 122, 124, 125, 126, 127, 130, 132, 134
Troy Memorial Stadium 11, 17, 30, 31, 34, 38, 44, 61, 78, 89
Troy-Piqua game 26, 34, 44, 50, 58, 77
Troy-Piqua rivalry 16, 17, 32, 37, 40, 41, 42, 47, 56, 60, 72, 86, 88, 93

U

Underwood, Scott 42, 43
University of Dayton 67, 75
University of Florida 41
University of Iowa 39, 110, 111
University of Michigan 37, 41, 112, 113, 114, 120, 131

INDEX

University of North
    Carolina 133
University of South
    Carolina 134, 135
University of Toledo 59
Upper Arlington 88
Urbana 22, 63
Urick, Max 34, 35,
    128, 129

V

Valentine, Harold 30
Vandalia 79
Vandalia-Butler 50, 63,
    67, 88, 89
Vanderbilt 90
Vaughn, Tom 35, 36,
    110, 126, 127, 128

W

Walker, Randy 41, 44,
    132, 133
Washington Redskins 116
Wayne 44, 62
Webster, Mike 114
Weebles 62
Welcome Stadium 68, 69
Wells, Leslie 24
Wertz Field 79
Wertz, George 15, 24,
    25, 26, 27, 28, 31,
    32, 33
Wertz Stadium 31, 49,
    50, 74, 83
West Carrollton 66, 79
Western Ohio League 42
Westerville North 53
Westerville South 90
Westfall, Bill 45, 46
"West Virginia Special" 44
White, Chris 42
White, T.J. 12, 90, 94
Widney, Dane 52
Williams, Isaiah 98

Williams, Joe 63, 65
Wise, Tom 42
Wolke, Joe 87, 88
Wright, Tyler 11, 13, 97

Y

Young, Scott 66, 75

Z

Zimpher, Bob 37

ABOUT THE AUTHOR

David Fong was born in Cincinnati, Ohio, but moved to Troy, Ohio, at the age of one. He graduated from Troy High School in 1992, having watched the Troy-Piqua rivalry from the stands. He began his first foray into sports journalism while in high school, working part time for his hometown newspaper, the *Troy Daily News*.

He went on to study journalism at The Ohio State University, where he was the beat writer for the Ohio State football team for Ohio State's school newspaper, the *Lantern*, in 1994. He served as the newspaper's sports editor in 1995 and 1996. Following an internship with the (Toledo) *Blade*, he graduated from The Ohio State University in 1996.

Four days following graduation, he began working full time in the sports department at the *Troy Daily News*, where he has been ever since.

David and his wife, Michelle, live in Troy with their two children, Sophia and Maximilian.

www.ingramcontent.com/pod-product-compliance
Lightning Source LLC
Chambersburg PA
CBHW042140160426
43201CB00021B/2357